D0513776

THE POCKET BOOK OF WEATHER

ENTERTAINING AND REMARKABLE FACTS ABOUT OUR WEATHER

MICHAEL BRIGHT

ADLARD COLES NAUTICAL

BLOOMSBURY

LONDON • NEW DELHI • NEW YORK • SYDNEY

Published by Adlard Coles Nautical
an imprint of Bloomsbury Publishing Plc
50 Bedford Square, London WC1B 3DP
www.adlardcoles.com

Conceived and produced by
Elwin Street Limited
144 Liverpool Road
London N1 1LA
www.elwinstreet.com

First published by Adlard Coles Nautical in 2013

ISBN 978-1-4081-8155-3

About the Author
Michael Bright is an executive producer with the BBC's Natural History Unit. He and his
colleagues are based in Bristol, England, but they trek around the world gathering material for
their groundbreaking television documentaries. Michael is the author of scores of books
about the natural world, from *The Private Life of Sharks* to *1001 Natural Wonders: You Must See
Before You Die*.

Contents

WEATHER
WORKS

What is weather?

We are all affected by the weather; from snowstorms on the slopes of the Rockies to the fogs of the Grand Banks, and from torrential rainstorms of India's monsoons to the droughts of the Sahel, the weather has an enormous impact on people, wildlife and the landscape.

Weather and climate

Weather is the result of movements and changes in the atmosphere – due to the uneven heating of the Earth's surface by the Sun – at a given time and place. Climate refers to meteorological conditions, including temperature, precipitation and wind, that characteristically prevail in a particular region.

Music of the spheres

Although weather is a mainly a phenomenon of the atmosphere, it has an effect on and is influenced by all the Earth's 'spheres'.

Atmosphere: *the body of air that envelops our planet, 99.9 per cent of which is below a height of 42 km (26 miles) from the Earth's surface, with the remainder stretching up to 1,000 km (620 miles) into space.*

Hydrosphere: *all the water – fresh and salt, solid, liquid or gas – on or close to the Earth, including oceans, rivers and moisture in the air.*

Lithosphere: *all the rocks and soil beneath our feet.*

Biosphere: *all the living organisms that live on or in the Earth.*

FACT

The atmosphere consists of 78.09 per cent nitrogen and 20.09 per cent oxygen, with other gases, such as argon, carbon dioxide, methane, neon, helium, krypton, hydrogen, xenon, ozone and water vapour, making up the rest.

All the spheres are closely connected, with changes in one sphere profoundly affecting another. Violent 'events', such as a hurricane or volcanic eruption, for example, can have a major impact on all the other spheres.

The atmosphere and the oceans redistribute energy and water constantly from the hot and humid tropics to the ice-cold poles.

Individual weather

Every place on the Earth has a climate and accompanying weather systems that reflect its actual location, for example next to the sea or in the centre of a land mass, perched high on a mountain chain or nestling in a valley, and adjacent to the Equator or close to the Poles.

Places closer to the Equator tend to have less 'seasonal' weather than those nearer the Poles. The tropics have wet and dry seasons (changes in humidity and rainfall), whereas temperate regions have distinct seasons – spring, summer, fall (autumn) and winter (changes in heating and cooling). This is because day length and the amount of solar energy is fairly constant in the tropics but varies throughout the year the further you are from the Equator. Regions inland also tend to have more extremes in climate and weather than places on the coast.

ABOVE The Earth's atmosphere from space. The atmosphere is divided into four sections – the troposphere, the stratosphere, the mesosphere and the thermosphere.

Land and sea

The way in which the energy from the Sun is absorbed at the Earth's surface depends on what is underneath – ocean or land. It is the energy trapped in these domains that primarily drives our weather systems, and less so the energy in the atmosphere itself.

Energy absorbed by the land: *Moves very slowly and, at a depth of only a few metres, there is little change throughout the year. If solar radiation increases, however, the land surface warms up rapidly, and if it decreases, such as in winter, the land cools significantly.*

Energy absorbed by the sea: *Enters the surface layers and is stored for long periods of time. The oceans have a great capacity for storing energy. This means that the sea responds more slowly to changes in solar radiation reaching the Earth's surface.*

ABOVE A satellite image of an anticyclone over Britain and western Europe. This weather phenomenon generally brings fair weather and clear skies.

Where the land meets the sea

Where land and sea are adjacent along coastlines, they heat and cool at appreciably different rates. This causes temperature and air pressure differences across the boundary between the two domains. In summer, when the land heats up rapidly, air moves from the sea to the land. In winter, when the land cools rapidly and the sea has retained its summer heat, the reverse occurs. This means that the distribution of the continents and oceans across the surface of the Earth has a considerable influence on global climate and seasonal climate cycles.

Stationary air masses

In the polar and tropical sectors of the world there are huge, semi-permanent high-pressure systems (anticyclones). These air masses hang about, showing little movement for long periods of time, which means a polar anticyclone is cool and a semi-tropical one is warm.

Air will flow out from these anticyclones in an attempt to reach energy equilibrium across the surface of the Earth. As it moves, it takes up more characteristics from the surfaces underneath.

Moving air masses

As air masses move over sea or land, they are influenced by their origin and the track that they take. Polar air moving southwards in the Northern Hemisphere (and northwards in the Southern Hemisphere) is likely to be cold. Air masses blowing over the sea are probably moist, while those blowing over the land are likely to be dry.

Categorisation of air masses

Air mass	Characteristics
Polar maritime	Cold and relatively moist
Polar continental	Cold and dry
Tropical maritime	Warm and moist
Tropical continental	Warm and dry

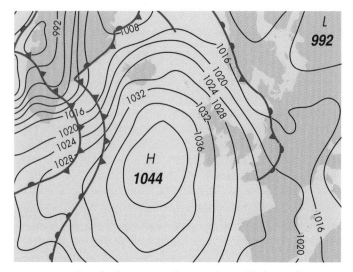

ABOVE A typical weather forecast map, showing isobars in black, warm fronts in red and cold fronts in blue. This map shows a large high-pressure system over the Atlantic Ocean.

Weather fronts

Weather fronts can be warm, cold or occluded (stationary). If warm air approaches and replaces cold air a **warm front** is formed. If cold air approaches and replaces warm air a **cold front** is formed. Cold fronts move faster than warm fronts, so if the former catches the latter and the warm air is pushed off the ground totally by the cold air, an **occluded front** is said to have formed. The fronts are not just at ground level but extend high up into the atmosphere.

Cold air is heavier and denser than warm, so as the lighter, warmer air rises above it, it gradually cools, water condenses and clouds are formed. This is why fronts are often associated with rain. On a weather map, a warm front is denoted by a line with red semicircles and a cold front by blue triangles. An occluded front has both. The direction of the semicircles and triangles shows which way the front is moving.

Air pressure

Air is heavy. It pushes down onto the ground and the force with which it does so is called 'air pressure'. There is a greater volume of air pushing down at sea level than on the top of a mountain so the air pressure at sea level is high, while on a mountaintop it is low.

Highs and lows

An area of **low pressure** is a mass of rising warm air that expands and cools, but cooler air cannot hold as much moisture as warm air so water vapour condenses and clouds are formed. A low-pressure system is, therefore, often accompanied by rain.

An area of **high pressure** is a mass of sinking air that warms as it approaches closer to the Earth's surface. Warm air holds more moisture, so areas of high pressure are often accompanied by good weather. Points of the same pressure are joined by '**isobars**', and on weather maps these appear as rings around high and low pressure systems.

Air flows directly between high- and low-pressure systems in an attempt to balance out the two pressures. This is how wind is created. Winds tend to blow from high pressure to low pressure, but because of the rotation of the Earth and friction with the surface below, they are diverted around the pressure systems.

In the Northern Hemisphere, winds blow anti-clockwise around a low-pressure system or cyclone and clockwise around a high-pressure system or anticyclone (and the opposite in the Southern Hemisphere). The greater the pressure difference between high and low pressure, the stronger the winds. On a weather map, isobars that are close together indicate strong winds.

FACT
Water boils at 100°C (212°F) at sea level, but at low pressure it boils at a lower temperature. On top of Mount Everest, 'boiling' water reaches a temperature of only 75°C (167°F).

Leisurely pressure

The anticyclone or high-pressure system is slow moving and can almost stop altogether. This is known as a 'blocking high', and it can force other weather systems to go round it. They are common over the Baltic Sea and Scandinavia, and sometimes in summer can mean weeks of beautiful, sunny weather. High-pressure systems are not always associated with fair weather, however. In winter, they can cause thick fogs and severe frosts.

Sometimes an area of high pressure is sandwiched between two low-pressure systems. This is known as a 'ridge' of high pressure and it often brings settled weather.

High-speed jet streams

Jet streams are narrow rivers of strong horizontal winds, blowing at over 50 knots (93 km/h or 58 mph), which are found above 6,000 m (20,000 feet) in the upper atmosphere. They not only manoeuvre storms but also determine where areas of high and low pressure are located. They form along the upper surfaces of warm and cold air masses.

As their tracks change, meteorologists watch them closely. During especially cold winter weather in the United States, for example, the jet stream can be over the Gulf of Mexico, while in summer it is over Canada.

There are several known jet streams but one of the most notorious is a stream that sometimes forms over Africa. At a height of 3,658–4,572 m (12,000–15,000 feet), it runs underneath the 15,240 m (50,000 feet) high Equatorial jet stream about 7° north of the Equator. Here violent thunderstorms arise that move across the Atlantic and develop into the full-blown hurricanes that devastate the Americas.

There are also '**jet streaks**' – high-altitude winds that move faster than the surrounding winds, and '**low-level jets**' – high-speed winds a few hundred metres above the Earth's surface.

Monsoon

The word 'monsoon' comes from the Arabic word *mausim*, meaning 'season'. In meteorological terms it is the seasonal reversal in the direction of the wind. It occurs in many countries of the world but the most well known is the Asian monsoon. It requires a large land mass and a vast ocean surface to function, and this it has with Bangladesh, India, Pakistan, Nepal, Sri Lanka, Thailand and Vietnam, the Arabian Sea and the Indian Ocean.

Asian monsoon

In autumn and winter, the Asian mainland temperature decreases, causing the wind to blow away from the land toward low pressure over the sea, creating the 'north-east monsoon'. In spring and summer the land warms up, causing a low-pressure system to form. With the land reaching temperatures of 45°C (113°F), up to 20°C (38°F) warmer than the sea, the winds then blow from the sea to the land, forming the 'south-east monsoon'. The south-east monsoon carries huge quantities of rain. This wet phase starts about 25 May when two arms of the monsoon – one through Sri Lanka and the other moving up from the Bay of Bengal – invade the mainland.

ABOVE A street in Varanasi, North Central India, during heavy monsoon rain.

World climates

In the early 1900s, the Russian-German climatologist Wladimir Peter Köppen introduced the most widely used classification system for world climates. He identified five classes and numerous subdivisions, though his findings can be summarised into three basic groups, with subdivisions corresponding to patterns of vegetation:

Low latitude climates
Close to the Equator – influenced by Equatorial tropical air masses.

Tropical moist climate: *Tropical rainforest with heavy rainfall all year, more than 250 cm (100 in), constant temperature of about 27°C (81°F) and humidity 77–88 per cent. Includes the Amazon Basin, Congo Basin and the East Indies from Sumatra to New Guinea.*

Wet-dry tropical climates: *Savannah with a very wet and a very dry season in India, Indochina, West Africa, southern Africa, parts of South America and northern Australia.*

Dry tropical climate: *Deserts in latitude 18°–28° in both hemispheres, regions close to the Tropics of Capricorn and Cancer, and occupying 12 per cent of the world's land surface, including south-west United States, Argentina, North Africa, Botswana, Namibia and central Australia.*

World climates and their associated biomes

Climate Type	Biome	Climate type	Biome
Moist tropical	Rainforest	Moist continental	Deciduous forest
Wet-dry tropical	Savannah	Boreal forest	Taiga
Dry tropical	Desert	Tundra	Tundra
Dry mid-latitude	Steppe	Highland	Alpine
Mediterranean	Chaparral		

BIOME: A major regional community of living organisms, such as grassland or desert, characterised by the dominant forms of plant life and the prevailing climate.

Mid-latitude climates

Temperate – influenced by both polar and tropical air masses.

Dry mid-latitude climate: *Barren grasslands with little or no trees ('steppe'), a semi-arid climate, warm summers and cold winters. Any drier and these regions would be desert, any wetter and they would be tall grass prairie; locations include western North America, central Europe and Eurasia.*

Mediterranean climate: *'Chaparral' vegetaion made up of drought-resistant shrubs and trees, with wet winters and extremely dry summers giving rise to frequent natural fires. Locations include lands bordering Mediterranean Sea, central and southern California, coastal West and South Australia, coastal Chile and tip of South Africa.*

Moist continental climate: *Deciduous forest in the battlefront between polar and tropical air masses, with abundant rain and snow throughout the year. Locations include eastern United States, southern Canada, northern China, Korea, Japan and central and eastern Europe.*

High latitude climates

Polar – where polar and continental air masses meet in the Arctic, but not in the Southern Hemisphere.

Boreal forest climate: *Coniferous forests ('taiga') with a continental climate of long cold winters and short, cool summers, including northern North America, Eurasia from Europe across Siberia to Pacific.*

Tundra climate: *Grasses, moss and heath growing in frozen soil ('tundra') along Arctic coast areas with a long and severe winter and a short mild season that is not a true summer. Locations include the Arctic regions of North America, Greenland coast and northern Siberia beside the Arctic Ocean.*

Highland climate: *Alpine cool and cold climate found in mountain and plateau areas, but with the same seasons as the surrounding region. Locations include Rocky Mountains, Andes, Alps, Himalayas, Mount Kilimanjaro in Africa and Mount Fuji in Japan.*

The seasons

The Earth tilts on its axis by 23.45°, and so during the course of the year the Sun's rays hit the Earth at different angles. Most energy is received when the Earth's surface is at right angles to the Sun, and this only happens between 23° North and South. Elsewhere it arrives at a shallower angle, the shallowest angles being closest to the Poles. In temperate regions, however, the changing angle gives us our seasons – spring, summer, autumn and winter, when different parts of the world are tilted toward the Sun at different parts of the year.

Solstice

The summer and winter solstices are the days on which the Sun reaches its furthest northern and southern declinations. The winter solstice, the shortest day in the Northern Hemisphere, is 21 or 22 December. The summer solstice, the longest day, occurs on 20 or 21 June. The reverse is true in the Southern Hemisphere.

FACT
Due to the elliptical shape of its orbit, the Earth is actually closest to the Sun during the northern winter, and furthest away around 3 July. This shows that the angle to the Sun is more important than the distance from the Sun.

Equinox

These are the days when day and night are equal. Two annual equinoxes occur when the Sun passes over the Equator. The vernal equinox occurs on 20 or 21 March, and is the beginning of spring in the Northern Hemisphere and of autumn in the Southern Hemisphere. The autumnal equinox occurs on 22 or 23 September.

WEATHER WATCHERS

The weather forecast

Do you watch the forecast on the television each evening, or look at the weather maps in the newspaper? The chances are that if you are a farmer, fisherman, gardener, long-distance traveller or a teacher with the prospect of 'wet playtime', your everyday life is influenced by changes in the weather and it is important to you to know what the heavens have in store for you. It is something that has preoccupied people for thousands of years, so the study of the weather – a science known as meteorology – has ancient roots.

The ancients

When prehistoric humans in the colder parts of the globe emerged from their caves each day, they probably did what you do every morning when you leave your house: they looked up at the sky and thought 'will it rain or will it shine?' The perceptions of warmth and cold, sunshine, wind, rain or snow must have been some of their earliest sensations. Eventually, they recognised signs and patterns in the sky and passed these observations on to successive generations, first by word of mouth and then in writing. These were the early weather forecasts, and they were recognised in the Bible.

When it is evening, ye say, It will be fair weather: for the sky is red. And in the morning, It will be foul weather today: for the sky is red and lowering.

St Matthew 16:2–3

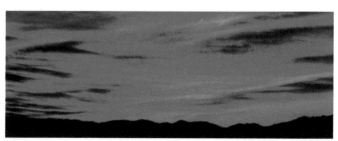

ABOVE A red sunset precedes fine weather – *red sky at night, shepherd's delight.*

Watch the sky... and the cat

Down the centuries, watching the behaviour of both wild and farmyard animals gave rise to short-range weather forecasts. Sayings and rhymes were once the only weather observations used to indicate what might happen in the following twenty-four hours.

If cows stand in a field it will be fine, if they lie down it will rain.

When bees stay close to the hive, rain is close by.

If crows fly low, wind's going to blow; If crows fly high, wind's going to die.

When seabirds fly to land, there truly is a storm at hand.

Flies will swarm before a storm.

Before a rainstorm: cats will clean and mew more; pigs wallow about and squeal; cows huddle together; horses 'switch and twitch' and sometimes bolt; insects fly low and bite; and birds chirp more loudly.

Similarly plants were good indicators.

Moss dry, sunny sky; Moss wet, rain you'll get.

When a rainstorm is approaching: dandelions close their blossoms tightly; morning glories tuck in their blooms as if ready for a sleep; clover folds up its leaves; and the leaves on many trees roll up or turn to show their undersides.

Weather soothsayers even tried longer-term predictions for weather in another season of the year.

When squirrels collect a big store of nuts, it will be a hard winter.

If the groundhog sees its shadow on 2 February, there'll be another six weeks of winter.

Fire, earth, air and water

For thousands of years humankind must have relied on folklore and myth to record the weather, but then along came the philosophers and scientists and the activity became more formalised.

The word 'meteorology' comes from Aristotle. He referred to heat and cold in terms of the four elements – fire, earth, air and water – but by 350 BCE he had already recognised the basics of what we now know as the hydrological cycle.

Aristotle's hydrological cycle

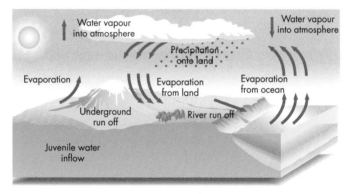

Now the Sun, moving as it does, sets up processes of change and becoming and decay, and by its agency the finest and sweetest water is everyday carried up and is dissolved into vapour and rises to the upper region, where it is condensed again by the cold and so returns to earth.

Aristotle (384–322 BCE)

First measurements

Crude measurements of rainfall were made in India about 400 BCE, using a container 46 cm (18 in) wide as a rain gauge. Rain gauges dating from the fifteenth century have been found also in Korea.

Early instruments

The first accurate meteorological measurements were taken in the seventeenth century.

Air pressure: *In 1643, the Italian physicist Evangelista Torricelli invented a barometer that could measure air pressure. Torricelli noticed that the weather changed as air pressure changed, a drop in pressure indicating a storm is coming and a rise in pressure predicting fair weather.*

Humidity: *Until 1655, observers relied on the moisture-absorbing properties of materials such as natural sponges, seaweeds and dried wool to measure humidity but that year Ferdinand II of Tuscany developed the hygrometer, which relied on the condensation of dew on an artificially cooled surface. Using this method, the amount of moisture in the atmosphere could be measured more accurately.*

Wind speed: *The Greeks recorded wind direction as far back as 100 BCE, but it was not until 1667 that Robert Hooke built an anemometer that measured wind speed reliably.*

Temperature: *Around the turn of the seventeenth century, Galileo Galilei invented the thermoscope, making the first rudimentary measurements of temperature; but it was not until 1714 that the German physicist Gabriel Fahrenheit developed the mercury thermometer.*

By the middle of the eighteenth century, science had the wherewithal not only to monitor accurately several different aspects of the weather, but also to predict what it was about to do.

FACT

Torricelli's barometer was something of an 'accidental invention', arising out of his experiments to prove that air actually has weight.

Meteorology is born

In 1765, French scientist Antoine-Laurent Lavoisier was one of the first to collect daily records that included measurements of air pressure, moisture content of the atmosphere and wind speed and direction. From the information he gathered, he claimed to be able to make weather predictions. 'With all of this information,' he said, 'it is almost always possible to predict the weather one or two days ahead with reasonable accuracy.'

The new science was given a boost in 1854, after a shipping disaster. A French naval ship and 38 merchant vessels were sunk in a violent storm near Balaklava in the Crimea. The director of the Paris Observatory was asked to investigate. He discovered that the storm had formed two days before the disaster and had moved across Europe from the south-east. Its arrival at Balaklava could have been predicted. This prompted the establishment of a national storm-warning system in France – probably the birth of the science of meteorology.

Global cooperation

Weather records were gathered first by amateur naturalists and recorded in personal diaries, but by the nineteenth century national meteorological services were established in Europe and later elsewhere. In 1853 an international conference on maritime meteorology agreed to exchange weather data in order to draw up the first weather maps, and by 1873 national services grouped together to form the International Meteorological Organisation (IMO). In 1950, after World War II, it was designated the World Meteorological Organisation (WMO) and by 1951, the United Nations recognised it as a specialised agency. As of 2004, 187 countries were members, enabling the free communication of standardised weather data for the purposes of forecasting the weather, as well as monitoring global climate changes and the long-range transmission of pollutants in the atmosphere.

FACT
The world's coldest temperatures of –88.3°C (–126.9°F) and –89.2°C (–128.6°F) were recorded at Vostok, Antarctica, on 25 August 1960 and 21 July 1983.

Temperature

Temperature is measured in the shade, not in direct sunlight, so the thermometer itself does not heat up and give a false reading. Temperatures in direct sunlight can be 10–15°C (18–27°F) higher than in the shade in still air, though this may be lower on windy days.

Maximum and minimum

The highest and lowest temperatures are recorded during the course of 24 hours by a special 'max and min' thermometer. The column of mercury or alcohol pushes tiny metal markers up and down inside the thermometer's tube. The bi-metallic dial type of thermometer has 'hands' that point to figures on a clock face.

ABOVE An iceberg in the Ross Sea, Antarctica – one of the coldest places on Earth.

FACT
The highest air temperature of 58°C (136°F) was recorded at El Azizia in Libya, Africa, on 13 September 1922.

Fahrenheit and celsius

Gabriel Fahrenheit published the first temperature scale in 1724. He assigned 0°F to the freezing point of a liquid (not simply water) that gave the lowest possible temperature at that time. The human body temperature was set at 98°F (actually 98.6°F) and the boiling point of water became 212°F.

Swedish astronomer Anders Celsius introduced the Centigrade (now known as Celsius) scale in 1742. It is based on the freezing and boiling points of water, divided conveniently into 100 divisions. This makes the freezing point of water 0°C and the boiling point 100°C.

Temperature conversion table

Celsius (°C)	Fahrenheit (°F)	Celsius (°C)	Fahrenheit (°F)	Celsius (°C)	Fahrenheit (°F)
−273.15	−459.67	−17.77	0	50	122
−200	−328	0	32	55	131
−180	−292	5	41	60	140
−160	−256	10	50	65	149
−140	−220	15	59	70	158
−120	−184	20	68	75	167
−100	−148	25	77	80	176
−80	−112	30	86	85	185
−60	−76	35	95	90	194
−40	−40	40	104	95	203
−20	−4	45	113	100	212

Some like it hot

The hottest temperatures on Earth are experienced in Ethiopia, Libya, Australia and the United States.

Dallol, Ethiopia: *The world's highest annual mean temperature was recorded in Dallol. Between October 1960 and December 1966, an average temperature of 35°C (94°F) was documented. Compare this with an average summer temperature for Key West, Florida, of 25.7°C (78.2°F).*

Death Valley, California: *On 43 consecutive days between 6 July and 17 August 1917, the average temperature was over 48°C (120°F) in Death Valley, California. A few years earlier, on 10 July 1913, the mercury reached 56.7°C (134°F). Death Valley is the lowest point on the Earth's land surface in the Western Hemisphere, and although the location is in mid-latitudes, the lower the altitude, the higher the temperature. The 209-km (130-mile) by 23-km (14-mile) desert has little more than 5 cm (2 in) of rain per year. It gets its name from one of 18 survivors from a party of 30 that was heading for the California gold fields in 1849.*

Marble Bar, Australia: *The world's longest hot spell spanned 162 consecutive days from 30 October 1923 to 7 April 1924 at Marble Bar, Western Australia, where the temperature was 38°C (100°F).*

Some have it cold

The coldest temperatures on Earth are experienced not only in the Antarctic, but also in north-eastern Siberia where the mercury can drop to -68°C (-90°F). The townsfolk of Verkhoyansk on the Yanu River and Omyakon on the Indigurka River often experience these icy temperatures. Both towns are surrounded by mountains far from the Arctic Sea, at latitudes of 63° North.

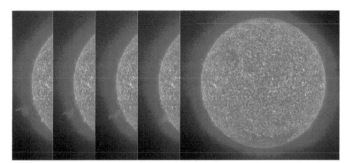

ABOVE An 'eruptive prominence' of gas from the Sun measuring more than 128,747 km (80,000 miles) long and 33,315°C (60,000°F).

FACT

The hottest air temperature experienced on Earth is 58°C (136°F). 150 million kilometres (93 million miles) away on the surface of the Sun the temperature is close to 5,538°C (10,000°F), and about 22,200°C (50,000°F) at its centre.

World air pressure

The average air pressure at sea level over the whole of our planet is 1,013.25 millibars. Due to the altitude on the top of high mountains, such as Mount Everest, the barometric air pressure is about one-third less than at sea level.

Low pressure

The lowest air pressure recorded on land was in a category 5 hurricane that hit the Florida Keys on 2 September 1935 – the Labor Day Storm. The barometer dropped to an unexpected 892.3 millibars. The railroad connecting Key West to the mainland was destroyed, every tree ripped from the ground and people were blasted by sand such that their clothes were stripped away.

Measuring from the ground

Manned weather stations on the ground monitor a whole host of factors – cloud height, speed and direction of movement, visibility, sunlight duration and intensity, maximum and minimum air temperature, soil temperature, atmospheric pressure, precipitation, humidity, wind speed and direction, pollution and pollen count, radiation from the Sun, space and the Earth itself and evaporation.

FACT
Eureka Weather Station at Slidre Fjord on Ellesmere Island in the Canadian High Arctic is about 1,130 km (702 miles) from the North Pole and considered to be the world's most remote manned weather station. In deepest winter, temperatures plunge regularly to -40°C (-40°F) and it's dark for 24 hours a day.

Untouched by human hand

The latest in weather monitoring is the Automated Weather Sensor System (AWSS), operated by the Federal Aviation Administration in the United States. Every minute, it records temperature, visibility, wind, precipitation, humidity, dewpoint, barometric pressure, cloud cover and the presence of thunder and freezing rain. This information is available instantly to airline pilots and weather offices providing the most accurate forecasts possible.

Weather radar

Weather radar produce pulsed signals that bounce off objects as small as raindrops and hail, providing data on precipitation and the movement of thunderstorm cells and wind shear events – changes in wind speed and/or direction over short distances. Smaller objects, such as water droplets and ice crystals in clouds, are detected by Millimeter Wave Cloud Radar, giving data on cloud thickness and height.

Measuring from the sky

Although ground-based observations are valuable for weather watchers, in order to obtain an overall view throughout the atmosphere other methods need to be employed.

Kites: *In 1749, Scottish meteorologists Dr Alexander Wilson and Thomas Melville attached thermometers to kites in order to monitor temperatures 915 m (3,000 feet) above the ground.*

First balloons: *In 1896, French meteorologist Leon Teisserenc de Bort began to attach instruments to balloons launched from his home in Versailles. In 1902 he revealed his discovery that the atmosphere consisted of two layers – the troposphere and stratosphere.*

Radio balloon: *In 1931, a balloon carried the first radio receiver and detectors (radiosonde) that transmitted weather data to the ground. In 1935 it was adopted as a routine activity first in Scandinavia.*

ABOVE *Vanguard* satellite, the first weather satellite, was launched 26 June 1958.

Weather balloons

Today, weather balloons filled with hydrogen or helium, with radiosondes attached, are tracked by Global Positioning System navigation satellites. They are considered to be the most effective way of gathering weather data from the upper atmosphere. They are flown twice a day from 1,100 sites around the world. A flight lasts for about two hours, the radiosonde reaching 40 km (25 miles) above the ground and drifting about 200 km (125 miles) from its release point. Temperatures in the region of -90°C (-130°F) are experienced up there, together with air pressure that is one-thousandth or less than that at the Earth's surface. As well as information about atmospheric pressure and humidity, special flights can also monitor ozone levels.

Whoosh!

Above 40 km (25 miles) solid fuel sounding rockets or elevator research rockets, which fly for 8–10 minutes, are used to obtain meteorological information. They usually take readings from altitudes of 50–200 km (31–124 miles) above the Earth's surface – the gap between balloons and satellites. European Space Agency (ESA) rockets take off from Kiruna in the north of Sweden and the National Space Administration's (NASA) sounding rockets go from Wallop on Virginia's eastern shore.

Earth from space

The first unofficial 'weather satellite' was NASA's *Vanguard II*, which took the first pictures from space of Earth's cloud cover. It was launched on 17 February 1959, but it was not until 1 April 1960 that *TIROS I* was put into orbit and it was established that satellites could monitor the Earth's weather patterns.

TOPEX/Poseidon was launched in August 1992, revolutionising our understanding of seasonal patterns in the world's oceans. The follow-up satellite, *Jason-1*, provided yet more data on ocean circulation and topography, enabling scientists to understand and predict the disruptive weather cycle known as 'El Niño'.

Forecast

Supercomputers are the key to today's weather forecasts. Data is taken from all over the world and fed into sophisticated software programs that simulate the atmosphere, from sea level to the highest altitudes. In order to predict what will happen, the atmosphere is divided up into 'cells' and as much data as possible is acquired from each cell. If predictions are short term, then data 'downwind' – where the weather systems are going – need only cover 160 km (100 miles) or so, but if a long-term forecast is required then global information is needed.

Accuracy

The complexity of the atmosphere and weather systems, and their chaotic behaviour, means that weather forecasts become less accurate the further ahead they try to predict. The accuracy of daily forecasts drops off significantly after 10 days, and even in the 5–10 day range errors can be large. Even highly visible events, such as hurricanes, can be difficult to predict. The predicted track of a storm five days away can be off as much as 587 km (365 miles) – the distance from Manchester to Penzance in England.

Unpredictable fluctuations

Small-scale fluctuations in the atmosphere, known as 'inertia-gravity waves', have an impact on the lower 16 km (10 miles) of the atmosphere. They can be seen, for example, as 'stripy' features in cloud and are the result of changes in fluids in the atmosphere. They can have a significant influence on weather prediction.

The forecast pioneer

English mathematician Lewis Fry Richardson made the first mathematical predictions about the behaviour of the atmosphere. In 1922, his laborious calculations in a pre-computer age meant that his results were not available until the weather system had passed. He concluded that his calculations would require the work of 60,000 people in order to provide a forecast before the event. Nevertheless the numerical system he developed has been used to the present day.

CLOUDS
AND FOG

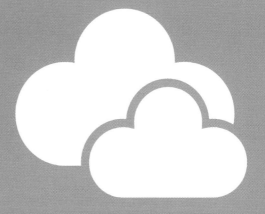

Clouds make weather

Clouds are important to climate systems. The Sun is always shining, but how much reaches the Earth's surface during the day depends on the amount and duration of cloud cover. The greater the cloud cover, the less solar energy reaches the Earth. This means the amount and type of clouds floating in the sky will control the amount of energy in the atmosphere. Clouds also transfer energy directly into the atmosphere. As water vapour condenses on the minute dust particles in clouds, energy is released.

Measuring cloud cover

Cloud cover is measured in units called *oktas*, each okta representing an eighth of the sky covered by cloud, as follows: clear sky, 1 okta, 2 oktas, 3 oktas, 4 oktas, 5 oktas, 6 oktas, 7 oktas and overcast.

It can be measured by anyone with a mirror. Divide the mirror into 16 squares using a chinagraph pencil or dark crayon and lay it on the ground in the open where the entire sky can be viewed and is not partly obstructed by buildings or trees. Then, count the number of squares with clouds in them. Divide this number by two to get the numbers of oktas – easy!

ABOVE A 'towering *cumulus*' cloud signals instability in the atmosphere, and possibly an approaching storm.

Remember: *If the Sun is overhead, do not look directly at it – not even in a mirror.*

Naming the clouds

Greek philosopher Theophrastus (c.373–287 BCE) described clouds as 'fleeces of wool', and French naturalist Jean-Baptiste Lamarck (1744–1829) categorised clouds as 'sweeping', 'bars' and 'flocks'; but in 1803, British amateur meteorologist Luke Howard (1772–1864) devised a simple cloud classification system. It was similar to the classification system used for plants and animals, created by the Swedish naturalist Carl Linnaeus (1707–1778), and used Latin names to describe the shape, appearance and thickness of clouds.

He described four main types of clouds: *cirrus*, meaning 'hair-like' and referring to wispy clouds; *cumulus*, meaning 'piled up' for lumpy clouds; *stratus*, meaning 'layer' for sheets of clouds; and *nimbus*, meaning 'cloud' to refer to low-level, grey, rain clouds. Other categories have been added since.

Latin cloud names	Meaning
Altos (alto)	Height
Capillatus	Having hair
Castellanus	Castle-like buttresses
Cirrus (cirro)	Lock, tuft or curl of hair
Congestus	Piled up
Cumuliform	Heaped
Floccus	Clumped
Fractus	Broken, ragged or irregular
Humilis	Flattened
Lenticularis	Lens-shaped (almond-shaped)
Mamma	Protuberance or udder
Nimbus	Rain cloud
Pileus	Cap or hood
Stratiform	Flattened

High-level clouds

Forming above 6,000 m (20,000 feet) where it is very cold, these clouds are composed mainly of ice crystals that are supercooled water droplets. High-level clouds are thin, wispy and white, although they can change to many different hues at sunrise and sunset.

Cirrus: *Occur mainly during fair weather, with tufts pointing in the direction of the air movement at the cloud's height. If there are strong winds the clouds have a hooked appearance.*

Cirrostratus: *Sheet-like, it can cover the entire sky and be several thousand metres thick yet completely translucent, and the only evidence of its presence might be a halo around the Sun or the Moon. Cirrostratus can thicken as a warm front approaches, and then become increasingly opaque, indicating that inclement weather associated with a warm front is approaching.*

Cirrocumulus: *Appears as rows of circular wisps or honeycomb-like ripples. It is one of the more rare cloud formations.*

ABOVE *Stratocumulus* clouds in the wake of a cold front passing through Brunswick, Georgia, USA.

Mid-level clouds

Appearing at 2,000–6,000 m (6,500–20,000 feet), these clouds are composed mainly of water droplets, although in especially cold weather they might contain ice crystals.

Altocumulus: *Clouds occur at this mid-level, and line up in parallel rows, ripples or in rounded masses. Part of the cloud is shaded grey, distinguishing it from the higher cirrocumulus cloud. They form as a result of thermal convection in unstable air layers, the lifting sometimes accompanying an approaching cold front. Altocumulus clouds forming on warm, humid days grow 'turrets' and are sometimes followed by high-level thunderstorms.*

Altostratus: *A thin layer of grey, milky cloud that can cover the entire sky. The Sun shines through, although the cloud often prevents shadows being cast, and it can be thick enough to obscure the Sun completely.*

Low-level clouds

Cloud base is generally below 2,000 m (6,500 feet), so these clouds are composed mainly of water droplets, although when the temperature plummets they can contain snow and ice crystals.

Nimbostratus: *A thick, dark cloud layer that can cover most of the sky, blotting out the Sun during the day and the Moon at night. It is usually associated with bad weather with falls of rain or snow depending on the season. Although sharing the sky with mid-level clouds, its base is in the low-level cloud layer.*

Stratocumulus: *Low and lumpy, with rounded cloud tops, and varying in colour from light to dark grey, with blue patches in between. It may be accompanied by light precipitation.*

Vertically developed clouds

These clouds are formed by thermal convection (hot air rising) or by frontal lifting, when air is lifted at weather front boundaries. They can be enormous and release huge quantities of energy as water droplets condense from water vapour inside the cloud.

Fair-weather cumulus: *Last for 40 minutes at most, and look like floating cotton. The top of the cloud marks the upper boundary of rising bubbles of air or thermals. Young clouds have well-defined boundaries, while older clouds appear ragged, due to evaporation and gradual disappearance of the cloud as the thermals that fuelled it become exhausted.*

Cumulonimbus: *Relatively benign cumulus clouds can develop into great dark and towering cumulonimbus clouds that harbour powerful thunderstorms, known as supercells. Cumulonimbus clouds are much larger than cumulus clouds and grow up to 12,000 m (39,372 feet) or more. They are fuelled by fast-moving updraughts, moving vertically in excess of 50 knots (93 km/h or 58 mph).*

Other cloud types

Billow clouds: *The top of these clouds resembles a series of waves breaking on the shore. They are formed in air flows with a marked vertical sheer but weak thermal layering.*

Mammatus: *Resembling pouches (or according to some observers – udders – hence the Latin name), these clouds form in sinking air, a rare occurrence. They look menacing but often follow rather than precede a thunderstorm.*

Orographic clouds: *These clouds often form along mountain ridges where the air has been forced upward simply by the shape of the land surface.*

Pileus: *These are smooth cap-like clouds often seen in association with high mountain peaks or towering cumulus clouds.*

Contrails: *Contrails or condensation trails resemble single streaks of cirrus-like cloud at high altitudes. Often, they are formed from dust and water vapour in the exhaust of engine gases.*

Cloud formation

Water exists in three states – liquid as in rain, solid as in ice and snow and as a gas known as water vapour. A mass of air must be moist, that is, contain large quantities of water vapour, before clouds can form. Most of this moist air moves in from the sea.

Clouds and fog form when a mass of warm, moist air expands and cools. As the air mass cools, its humidity rises, and when it reaches 100 per cent, water vapour condenses to form tiny water droplets that attach to dust, salt or other airborne particles, which in these circumstances are known as 'condensation nuclei'. If a cloud has a long life, the droplets will eventually fall as rain.

ABOVE An unusual contrail breaks through a beautiful sunrise.

Clouds form as air cools. This cooling is usually due to an air mass rising, which is caused by either convection, convergence or lifting.

Convection: *A vertical movement of air. When the Sun warms the Earth's surface, 'bubbles' of warmed air, known as thermals, float upwards. As long as the air mass is warmer than the surrounding air, it will continue to rise. Eventually, it reaches the point where it cools, and water vapour condenses to form a cloud. This is the way in which fair weather cumulus and cumulonimbus clouds are formed.*

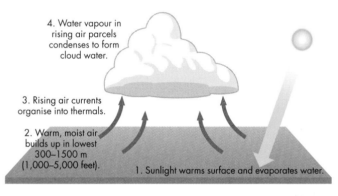

4. Water vapour in rising air parcels condenses to form cloud water.

3. Rising air currents organise into thermals.

2. Warm, moist air builds up in lowest 300–1500 m (1,000–5,000 feet).

1. Sunlight warms surface and evaporates water.

Convergence: *Occurs where masses of air converge horizontally on the Earth's surface, and since they cannot go downward they must rise. Where they rise, the air pressure at the point of convergence decreases, forming a low-pressure system. This upward movement is on a smaller scale than with convection, so the clouds generated are less vertical.*

Lift from weather fronts: *Occurs across the boundaries of weather fronts. At a cold front, the mass of cold air pushes up the warm air ahead of it. As the air rises, water condenses and clouds are formed. The rise is so steep and vigorous that rain showers and even thunderstorms develop. At a warm front, which moves more slowly than a cold front, the rise of warm air is on a gentler slope so the rain ahead of the front is more persistent.*

FACT
A modest-sized cloud, say, 1 km (0.6 miles) in diameter and 100 m (330 feet) thick has the same mass as a Boeing 747 jumbo jet, and a large cumulonimbus storm cloud 10 km (6 miles) tall with a cloud base 10 km (6 miles) in diameter is the same mass as 10,000 jumbo jets.

Lift from topography: *If a moving air mass is confronted by a mountain or mountain chain, again it cannot go down so it rises up. It cools as it rises, forming clouds.*

Rain clouds, snow clouds, storm clouds

Rain often starts as snow. The clouds in which water droplets condense are so high and so cold that the temperature is below freezing and the water freezes instantly to form ice crystals. As the ice crystals fall, they gather others around them to form snowflakes. If the air temperature below the cloud is above freezing point, they melt and fall as rain, but if the air temperature on the ground is at or below freezing they fall as snow.

Storm clouds are dark because they are denser than 'fluffy' clouds and prevent the light from shining through.

Night cloud blanket

Although we may think that the cloud layer acts as a blanket at night to keep in the day's heat, in fact, it does not. The water droplets in clouds absorb infrared energy, which is then radiated in all directions, some lost to space and some radiated back to Earth.

Cloud seeding rainmakers

In 1946, Vincent J. Schaefer was working with a chilled chamber at the laboratories of General Electric, in Schenectady, New York. On one occasion, he thought the chamber was too warm and placed dry ice inside. A cloud formed around the dry ice shavings, indicating that water vapour in the chamber had condensed around the dry ice crystals to form water droplets. This is the basis of the 'cold rain' process – the creation of additional nuclei around which water vapour can condense.

Cloud seeding can be achieved either by airplanes flying through clouds to introduce foreign particles that act as precipitation nuclei, or by generators on the ground that pump airborne particles into the lower atmosphere. Silver iodide is used during cloud seeding as its properties are similar to those of ice crystals. In the tropics, a 'warm rain' process is used in which a smoke of calcium chloride provides the additional 'hygroscopic' nuclei. Seeding from silver iodide burners, dry ice pellets or hygroscopic flares is conducted from aircraft.

The effectiveness of cloud seeding is difficult to assess, as precipitation is inconsistent. Rainfall from seeded clouds, however, is thought to last longer than from unseeded clouds. It also covers a wider area and precipitation is higher.

By comparing historical levels of rain or snow and the figures obtained post-seeding, claims have been made that there is between 5 per cent and 30 per cent increase in precipitation after seeding.

FACT
China has about 30 modified aircraft, 6,900 anti-aircraft guns and 3,800 rocket launchers assigned to cloud-seeding duties. Even so, regions appear to compete for clouds that are sailing overhead, and will complain if their neighbours receive significantly more precipitation.

FACT
'Snow cannons' create extra snow at ski resorts by combining water with compressed air, causing the water to atomise into tiny droplets that then crystallise into snow.

Strange clouds

Hole-in-the-cloud

On 23 February 1968, an unusual cloud formation appeared over Vandenberg Airforce Base, California. It was an almost perfectly circular hole in cirrocumulus cloud. Similar holes were seen in clouds near Corpus Christi, Texas. Experts suggest the phenomena could be the result of seeding, either intentionally from aircraft or from a rocket test, or naturally from debris, perhaps from a meteorite. To this day, however, the round holes remain a mystery.

Cloud mystery solved

In the late 1960s, pictures of the Earth from satellites showed lines of clouds for which meteorologists could find no explanation. They were seen commonly off the California coast in late spring and early summer. A United Airlines' pilot solved the mystery when he was able to observe the phenomenon up close; the cloud line he observed was caused by a condensation trail, not from an aircraft, but from a ship. A trail from the ship's smokestack caused a cloud line to extend up to 240 km (150 miles) before fading out.

Noctilucent clouds

These are pearly white clouds made of ice crystals that form in cold periods during the summer in polar regions. They occur at latitudes 60°–70° North and South and at high altitudes – about 80 km (50 miles) high. They are illuminated by the Sun long after sunset and, therefore, appear luminous in the dark.

FACT
On average, the concentration of cloud condensation nuclei – the small particles on which the droplets of water in clouds form, such as dust – is 100 to 200 million per m³ of air (3–6 million per cubic foot).

Fog and mist

Fog and mist are composed of millions of miniature water droplets suspended in air – basically clouds close to the ground. Fog is denser than mist as it contains more water droplets. The classification, however, depends on what you are driving. Aircraft pilots have difficulty if they cannot see further than 1 km (3,300 feet), whereas motorists hit fog when they cannot see more than 200 m (660 feet).

All at sea

The waters around the Avalon Peninsula, Newfoundland, and over the nearby Grand Banks in the Atlantic Ocean, are considered to be among the foggiest places in the world. Argentia, on the western side of the peninsula, claims the title with 206 foggy days recorded in 1966. Other foggy sites include Belle Island and Cape Race with over 160 days.

Fog, sometimes called sea smoke, forms when warm moist air blows up from the south and hits the cold, iceberg-laden Labrador Current that flows down from the north. Fogs can occur in all seasons but are more frequent in spring and early summer. It can be so thick that it is not dispersed by strong winds.

On average, however, the Grand Banks experience about 120 days of fog per year. It is at the southern extremity of 'Iceberg Alley', the watery grave of the RMS *Titanic* and the location of *The Perfect Storm*.

Formation of fog

Fog can form in several different ways, but generally fog builds when very moist air, close to the ground, is cooled so the water vapour in the air condenses.

Ground or radiation fog: *This is formed when heat rising from the ground cools after sunset.*

Advection fog: *This develops when warm moist air moves over a colder surface, cooling the air. Arctic sea smoke, a form of sea fog, is an example of an advection fog.*

Upslope fog: *Forms when warm, moist air is pushed up by a topographical feature, such as mountains.*

Precipitation or frontal fog: *Common after a storm. After the rain has evaporated and more water vapour fills the air, it condenses to produce a fog.*

ABOVE Sea fog, part of the stratus cloud family.

San Francisco fogs

Each summer, the harbour and approaches of San Francisco Bay are blanketed with a dense fog. This is because the inshore waters along this coast are significantly colder than those offshore. Warm moist air blows from the warm Pacific offshore waters and is transported by westerly winds over the cooler waters that hug the coast. The air temperature drops and fog is formed.

The pogonip

In the mountains of the Nevada Sierras, a frozen fog – the 'pogonip', a native American word meaning 'icy fog' or 'white death' – appears during the winter months, even on clear, bright days. In the blink of an eye, the air can be filled with floating needles of ice. It is said that to breathe the pogonip is to bring death to the lungs, and when it appears people rush for cover. It is caused when moisture in the air is frozen suddenly around the summits of high mountains. It manifests itself when trees, houses and anything in the open turn white without apparent cause. The minute crystals of ice attach to anything in sight, including the hair and clothing of people, to produce what one observer described as a 'grotesque effect'.

Burning fog

In 1758, a letter to *The Annual Register* – an annual survey of the previous year, published in the United Kingdom, that traditionally focused on history, politics and literature – described how a strange fog descended on Kensington, Connecticut. It came in thick clouds, 'striking against houses' and resembled a 'thick steam rising from boiling wort'. It was accompanied by such a heat that the observer thought his house was on fire. Other people came from their dwellings, thinking the 'world was on fire, and the last day had come'. What caused the burning fog remains a mystery.

RAIN

What is rain?

Rain is water falling in drops from water vapour that has cooled and condensed in the atmosphere. Each raindrop resembles a homemade hamburger in shape, for as it falls the bottom is pressed flat and the top remains rounded. Raindrops with a diameter of less than 0.5 mm are known as drizzle.

What triggers rain?

There are two recognised processes by which rain is caused to fall.

Collision and wake capture

In a cloud, there are so-called 'super-condensation nuclei' that attract more condensed water vapour and grow larger than the others. These might be natural sea salt, sulphuric acid from volcanoes or even industrial exhausts. As they grow larger the air currents are no longer able to hold them up and they start to fall. They bump into others as they fall, causing a chain reaction, and behind each large droplet is a partial vacuum that sucks in smaller droplets. This is probably the way rain forms in relatively low-level clouds that are below the freezing level.

Bergeron process

Clouds that extend into the freezing zone, such as huge cumulus clouds, sometimes contain liquid water droplets. These supercooled droplets turn to ice crystals when the temperature reaches -35°C (-31°F), giving the cloud a fibrous appearance like the tops of cumulonimbus clouds. As the crystals fall they collide with others and gather increasingly more ice to form snowflakes. If the surface temperature is below freezing they fall as snow; if it is above freezing they fall as rain.

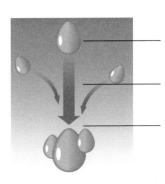

COLLISION AND WAKE CAPTURE

Water droplet becomes too heavy to remain suspended in the cloud, and starts to fall.

As droplet falls, smaller droplets are drawn toward it by the partial vacuum that forms in its wake.

Droplet collides with other droplets and grows in size during its descent.

Categorising rain

There are three main types of rain:

Frontal rain: *Rain falling at the boundary between warm and cold air masses.*

Convective rain: *Rain that falls when warm air rising from the ground cools, often producing thunderstorms.*

Orographic rain: *Rain that falls when an air mass is forced to rise above features in the landscape, such as mountains.*

Rain and rain shadows

When a moist air mass is forced upward by a mountain, it cools at a rate of 3°C (5.4°F) for every rise of 1,000 m (3,281 feet). Water vapour condenses and light orographic rain and drizzle falls on the windward side of the mountain.

Closer to the summit, torrential orographic rain falls, with the air mass losing much of its moisture content.

On the lee slopes – the sheltered slopes – the rain is lighter and as the air descends (causing a Föhn wind) it warms at a rate of 9.8°C (17.64°F) per drop of 1,000 m (3,281 feet).

Further from the mountain less rain falls, until it stops altogether and a 'rain shadow' is experienced.

Rainfall intensity classifications

Type of rain	Definition
Very Light	Scattered drops do not completely wet a surface
Light	Greater than a trace and up to 2.54 mm (0.10 inches) per hour
Moderate	Rate of fall is between 2.794 mm (0.11 inches) and 7.62 mm (0.30 inches) per hour
Heavy	Rain falling at a greater rate than 7.62 mm (0.30 inches) per hour

Intensity and duration are usually inversely related. High-intensity rainstorms are of short duration, and low-intensity storms are of long duration. Intensity and area are also related in that less rainfall can be expected over a larger area than a smaller one. High-intensity storms have larger raindrops than low-intensity storms.

Rain records

Several sites compete for the title 'wettest place on Earth':

Hawaii: *Harbours one of the world's ultra-wet places – Mount Waialua on Kauai. On its slopes, a weather station at an altitude of 1,569 m (5,148 feet) records on average 11.68 m (38 feet, 4 inches) to 13 m (42 feet, 8 inches) of rainfall per year, and it rains 335–360 days of the year.*

Cherrapunji: *Located in the state of Meghalaya, India, it has the highest rainfall recorded during the course of one year. From August 1860 to August 1861, 26.46 m (86 feet, 10 inches) fell. On a shorter timescale, 3.72 m (12 foot, 2.5 inches) fell between 12 and 15 September 1974. Long-term figures, however, indicate its neighbour, Mawsynram, is wetter with an average of 11.87 m (39 feet) per year compared to Cherrapunji's 10.82 m (35 feet, 6 inches).*

Wet days

Reunion: *Holds the world record for the most rain falling in a 24-hour period. The town of Foc-Foc on the Indian Ocean island recorded 1,825 mm (71.85 inches) on 6 to 7 January 1966 – that's 1.8 m (6 feet)!*

United States: *The wettest day occurred at Alvin, Texas, on 26 July 1979. In 24 hours, 1,092 mm (43 inches) fell on the town. The second wettest day was in Yankeetown, Florida, where 983 mm (38.7 inches) fell on 5 September 1950.*

United Kingdom: *The most rain recorded in a single day was 279.4 mm (11 inches) at Martinstown, Dorset, on 18 July 1955. Two people were killed during the downpour. Scotland's rainiest day was 17 January 1974, when 238 mm (9.37 inches) fell in 24 hours at Sloy Main Adit, Loch Lomond.*

New Zealand: *The wettest 24-hour period was 21 to 22 January 1984, when 682 mm (26.85 inches) fell on Colliers Creek, 473 mm (18.62 inches) of it falling in a 12-hour period on the 22nd. Its wettest hour, however, was at Whenuapai on 16 February 1966, when 107 mm (4.213 inches) fell in 60 minutes, and its wettest 10 minutes was on 17 April 1948, when 34 mm (1.339 inches) fell at Tauranga.*

Australia: *The wettest 24 hours occurred on 2 February 1893, when 906.8 mm (35.7 inches) of rain fell at Beewah, Queensland.*

Canada: *The wettest day was 6 October 1967, when 489.2 mm (19.6 inches) fell in 24 hours on Ucluelet Brynnor Mines in western British Columbia.*

Asia: *The wettest day was recorded on 15 July, 1911, when 1,168 mm (45.98 inches) of rain fell in 24 hours at Baguio on the island of Luzon, Philippines.*

Dry as a bone

While some places on Earth are prone to heavy rainfall, others are characterised by extreme lack of rain. This normally occurs because of a 'rain shadow', which describes the area behind a mountainous barrier, with respect to the prevailing wind direction. Any moist air that might approach the area is lifted up over the mountains, in the process cooling and losing all its moisture as precipitation.

Driest town on Earth: *Arica, in Chile's Atacama Desert, receives no more than 1 mm (0.04 inches) of rain on average per year, and for 14 consecutive years it has had no rain at all.*

A dry spell: *The longest dry spell in the United States occurred at Bagdad, California. The rain stopped on 3 October 1912 and it failed to rain again until 9 November 1914, a total of 767 days of drought.*

ABOVE The Atacama Desert is so dry because it is blocked from moisture by the Andes on one side and the Pacific coastal range on the other.

Flash floods

Flash floods are huge bodies of fast-moving water that sometimes follow extremely heavy, localised rainfall. They can transform a dry stream bed or even a city street into a raging torrent in seconds. Their impact can be devastating, as the sheer force of the water is unexpected. A flash flood no more than 15 cm (6 inches) deep can sweep you off your feet, and one 60 cm (2 feet) deep can move parked cars.

31 May 1889: *Torrential rains caused the South Fork Dam to break, and a flash flood engulfed the town of Johnstown, Pennsylvania, United States, killing 2,200 people. It was one of the worst disasters in US history.*

15 and 16 August 1952: *Over night, 35 people were killed and hundreds lost their homes when a flash flood containing an estimated 81 million tonnes of boulder-strewn water washed down the East and West Lyn rivers from Exmoor at 320 km/h (200 mph) and destroyed the fishing village of Lynmouth in North Devon, England. Over 23 cm (9 inches) of rain had fallen on the moor, over an area made famous in R. D. Blackmore's* Lorna Doone.

9 and 10 June 1972: *237 people were drowned in a flash flood at Rapid City, South Dakota, United States.*

FACT
On August 14 1987, a thunderstorm dumped 9.35 inches (237.5 mm) of rain on Chicago's O'Hare Airport in 18 hours, the largest 24-hour record in the city's history. Floods closed the airport, the first time it has been shut down by the weather outside of winter.

26 January 1974: *Brisbane, in Queensland, Australia and the surrounding areas received 82 cm (32 inches) of rain over a five day period. The resulting flooding took the lives of 16 people and 8,000 were left homeless.*

14 August 1975: *A very localised downpour hit Hampstead, London, and dumped 17 cm (6.7 inches) in just 155 minutes. The run-off was extraordinary with streets becoming rivers, the Underground subway system was flooded and brought to a standstill, manhole covers shot out of the ground under the intense water pressure and basements filled with water. One man was trapped in his apartment and drowned. Just half a kilometre or so away the rainfall was less than 5 mm (0.2 inches).*

1 October 1976: *Torrential rain carried by Hurricane Lisa caused a dam to burst on the Cajoncito River and 630 people were killed by the surge of water that hit La Paz, Mexico.*

6 June 1981: *A flash flood demolished a railway bridge at Bihar, India, causing a packed train to crash. Over 800 people were killed in what is considered to be one of the world's worst train disasters.*

2 November 2003: *A 12-metre (40-foot) high flash flood swept down the Baharok River in North Sumatra, Indonesia. 250 people were reported missing, but only 83 bodies were recovered from beneath the logs and mud and 1,200 familes were left homeless.*

FACT

An extraordinary amount of energy is tied up in a falling raindrop. Scientists have worked out that in a place with an average annual rainfall of about 700 mm (28 inches) the total amount of energy released on impact with the ground is the equivalent of 3,600 tonnes of high explosive.

Coloured rain

Red

Between 21 and 23 February 1903, so-called 'red rain' fell over the southern half of England and Wales. The colour was thought to have come from the Sahara, south of Morocco, where dust was scooped up by a strong north-east wind and carried aloft. It travelled around the western side of an anticyclone (high-pressure system) centred on Spain and Portugal, crossed over the Azores and fell as red rain, dumping an estimated 9 million tonnes of dust.

Yellow

On 14 February 1870 a yellow rain containing particles of cobalt blue, pearly corpuscles, fungal spores and microscopic planktonic organisms fell on Genoa, Italy, and on 27 February 1877 a golden-yellow rain containing minute things shaped like 'arrows, coffee beans, horns and discs' fell on Peckloh, Germany. While the most obvious explanation

ABOVE A four-wheel-drive struggles through a flash flood in northern Australia.

for the yellow colour in rain is pollen from coniferous trees, the variety of strangely-shaped particles described is difficult to explain.

Black

On 20 January 1911, black rain fell on Switzerland and on 14 August 1888 a 'shower of ink' fell at the Cape of Good Hope, both places relatively remote from factory chimneys.

On 14 January 1862 black rain fell in Aberdeenshire, Scotland, and all along the coast of the county. At 8 a.m. in the morning the sky was clear, but as it darkened and threatened rain, a huge, dense, black cloud 'came driving over the sea' from the southeast and 'discharged a shower of rain with drops like ink'. Smoke from factories was the obvious explanation, even though the weather system had arrived from over the sea, but it was doubted whether a sufficient quantity of soot could be distributed through the atmosphere to produce the blackness described. Another suggestion was an eruption of the volcano Vesuvius in Italy, but that volcano is a considerable distance away, so the actual explanation remains unknown.

Point rainfall

2 August 1966: *An amateur meteorologist at Greenfield, in southern New Hampshire, United States, recorded an unusually high rainfall reading, whereas his neighbour just 0.5 km (0.3 miles) away observed nothing. The rain began at 7 p.m. in the evening and was torrential until past 10 p.m. 'The noise on the roof was terrific,' he recalled, 'and stone and gravel were being washed away by torrents of water.' In the morning, he discovered the heavy rain had fallen on an area just 1.6 km (1 mile) in diameter and nowhere else.*

1 August 1932: *An eyewitness to a localised downpour was in Bayswater, London, when torrential rain fell only 90 m (300 feet) from where he was standing. It was so intense a layer of spray as high as a taxi wheel advanced toward him and then receded. Where he was standing, however, just a few drops had fallen.*

Crackling rain

The year was 1892 and the place Cordoba in Spain. On a warm and windless day, an electrical engineer witnessed a flash of lightning followed by an unusual fall of rain. As the raindrops hit the ground, trees and walls, they crackled and emitted sparks of light.

Rain without clouds

18 July 1925: *An amateur weatherwatcher in Bovisand, near Plymouth, England, experienced a local shower from a cloudless sky. The rain covered an expanse of concrete no more than 17 m (60 feet) square.*

20 January 1935: *Drizzle fell for about ten minutes from a cloudless sky at Benson, Oxfordshire, England. The Sun was shining and a faint rainbow was visible through the falling rain.*

On several occasions: *An observer at Grayshott, Hampshire, England, recorded drizzle from cloudless skies. On 29 December 1929, a clear evening followed a stormy day. The stars were shining and not a cloud was seen, yet a noticeable drizzle fell for a few minutes. Again, in January 1931, a cloudless evening at sunset produced a significant amount of rain. And, on 3 January 1933, light drizzle occurred some time after clouds had disappeared from the sky.*

FACT

In imperial measurements, one inch of rain falling over an area of one acre has a weight of one ton. In metric terms, 25 mm falling on 0.4 hectares weighs about 0.9 tonnes. Across the entire world, one billion tons of rain falls every minute. If you live in a place with high rainfall, you may be hit by as many as 50 million rain drops every year.

See a rainbow

In very general terms, a rainbow is produced when light from the Sun is bent (refracted) as it passes through the air into and through a raindrop, and is broken down (dispersion) into all its possible visible colours (wavelengths) – red, orange, yellow, green, blue, indigo and violet. The rays at different wavelengths exit the raindrop in slightly different directions so the colours are separated into bands. A rainbow is curved partly because raindrops are curved, and partly because the raindrops bend the sunlight over an angle. This gives a circular bow (actually half-a-circle because rain cannot be below the ground) where the shadow of your head should be. The bow is relative to the observer, so your view of a rainbow is unique. Nobody else can see a rainbow as you can. You can see a rainbow when the rain is directly in front of you and the Sun is directly behind.

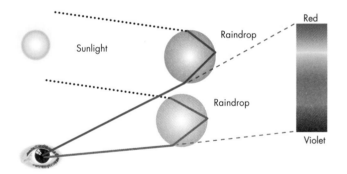

Rainbow twins

There are actually many rainbows, but you cannot see them all. A secondary rainbow, at an angle of 51°, is sometimes seen inside the primary rainbow, but the colours are reversed. Tertiary and other rainbows are very pale.

There is no end to a rainbow. The rainbow moves as you move, so you will probably never find that fabled pot of gold.

HAIL AND SNOW

Freezing rain

Freezing rain consists of supercooled water droplets that freeze on contact with the ground, forming a glaze of slippery ice. Roads are so icy they become impassable, and the build-up of ice on telephone lines and power cables can become so heavy it brings them down.

Freezing rain usually forms as a narrow band of rain on the cold side of a warm front, where warm air is sandwiched between colder air above and below. The air above and ground below has temperatures at or below freezing. The rain begins falling as snow in the upper cold layer, but on leaving the cloud it meets a layer of relatively warm air and melts into conventional rain that continues to fall. The temperature closer to the surface is at or below freezing, but the rain itself does not freeze; it is said to be 'supercool'. When the supercooled drops hit the ground, power cables, trees or anything in the open, they freeze instantly, forming a thin layer of ice.

Ice storms

Ice storms deposit two types of ice:

Glaze ice: *Transparent and homogeneous layers of ice that lie on horizontal and vertical surfaces are known as 'glaze'.*

Rime ice: *Milky and crystalline ice, resembling sugar, is 'rime'. It is less dense, less persistent and causes less damage.*

FACT
Freezing rain is extremely dangerous. People can fall down steps or on pavements, or getting out of their cars, causing serious injury and even paralysis. Automobiles can go totally out of control, with multi-car pileups and fatal traffic accidents on roads like skating rinks.

Ice storm Canada

In January 1998, southern Quebec and New Brunswick in Canada and New England in the United States were hit by five days of the worst ice storm in living memory. Some areas received over 120 mm (4.7 inches) of freezing rain, more than double that normally experienced in this region. It hit forests badly, causing widespread die-off of deciduous trees, especially sugarbush from which maple syrup is obtained. It has taken several years to recover. Evergreens stood up better to the extra loading; a 15 m (50 foot) conifer can carry as much as 45,000 kg (99,000 pounds) of ice.

The impact on the local area and people was considerable. Three weeks after the '98 Ice Storm, 700,000 houses were still without power. About 120,000 km (75,000 miles) of power and telephone cables were brought down, and damage was so severe in southern Quebec that entire sections of the grid had to be rebuilt rather than repaired. Over 100,000 people sought refuge in shelters, and 25 people were killed.

ABOVE Power and telephone lines sagging under the weight of ice from an ice storm. This effect brings people into dangerous proximity with live electrical currents.

Hail – falling ice

Hail originates in towering convective clouds, such as cumulonimbus, where supercooled water droplets aggregate around dust particles or other hail in the process of forming. The water freezes around the particle, but the particle does not necessarily fall. It can be blown about inside the cloud gathering more water and increasing in size. Therefore, the longer hail remains in the cloud, the bigger it becomes. Eventually, it becomes too big for the air mass to support and it drops. It appears usually as rounded, but sometimes irregular-shaped, pieces of ice. Its structure, if sliced in two, is like an onion with clear and opaque layers. It is classed as 'hail' if the diameter of the pieces is more than 5 mm (0.2 inches), each lump known as a hailstone. Smaller pieces are known as 'ice pellets', 'snow pellets', or 'graupel'.

Ice pellets

These are pieces of ice less than 5 mm (0.2 inches) in diameter, and arrive in two forms – hard grains of frozen raindrops or melted and refrozen snowflakes, and pellets of snow encased in ice. They bounce when they hit the ground and are more commonly referred to as 'sleet'.

Snow pellets

Snow pellets are frozen precipitation consisting of small, opaque, white, round or conical grains of ice with a diameter between 2 mm (0.08 inches) and 5 mm (0.2 inches). Unlike hail, they break up when they hit the ground. They are known also as 'small hail' or 'soft hail'.

Graupel

This is frozen precipitation with snowflakes or ice crystals combined with supercooled water and frozen together.

Hail thunderstorm

Hail often accompanies thunderstorms, frequently along a cold front where the air above is much colder than that at the bottom. Updraughts in the thundercloud keep the hail aloft and individual hailstones can grow to an enormous size. Hail can also occur in tropical regions, where severe and supercell thunderstorms have very strong updraughts. Hail can fall, therefore, in summer when there may not be a cold front.

Expensive damage

In recent times, extreme hailstorms have hit several cities with expensive consequences:

11 July 1990: *Hailstones the size of cricket balls fell on Denver, Colorado, United States, with an estimated US$625 million worth of damage to roofs and automobiles.*

5 May 1995: *Dallas and Fort Worth, Texas, United States, spent US$2 billion in repairs following hailstorms.*

12 April 1999: *Sydney, Australia, experienced AU$190 million of damage and many people were injured.*

19 July 2002: *25 people died and hundreds were seriously injured in freak hail conditions in China's Hennan Province.*

FACT

The worst human and environmental damage from a reported hailstorm occurred at Munich, Germany on 12 July 1984. Entire fields of crops were destroyed, bark was stripped from trees, 70,000 buildings had roofs pockmarked with holes, 250,000 cars were bombarded by ice and 400 people were badly hurt. The bill came to an estimated £6 million.

Record hailstones

Hailstones are short-lived so accurate measurements are difficult to attain, making record holders impossible to verify. As a result, the world's biggest hailstone has been claimed in several locations.

6 July 1928: *In Potter, Nebraska, United States, a record-breaking hailstone fell. It was 17.8 cm (7 inches) in diameter and weighed 0.68 kg (1.5 pounds). This record lasted for over 40 years, before the 1970 Coffeyville hailstone (see below) took its place.*

5 September 1958: *The largest recorded hailstone in the British Isles landed at Horsham, West Sussex, on 5 September 1958. It weighed 142 g (5 ounces).*

3 September 1970: *A hailstone fell in Coffeyville, Kansas. It measured 14.5 cm (5.67 inches) in diameter, 44.5 cm (17.5 inches) in circumference and weighed 760 g (1.67 pounds), the heaviest on record in the United States.*

14 April 1986: *A hailstone reported to weigh 1 kg (2.25 pounds) landed in the Gopalanj district of Bangladesh. According to the* Guinness Book of Records *(1994), the hailstorm killed at least 92 people and injured many more.*

June 22 2003: *A hailstone with a diameter of 17.8 cm (7 inches), a circumference of 47.6 cm (18.7 inches), and weighing 0.59 kg (1.3 pounds) landed at Aurora, Nebraska. The quick-thinking local residents who found the hailstone immediately preserved it in a freezer so it could be measured. About 40 per cent of the hailstone was lost when it hit a roof, however, and it had melted somewhat before measurements could be taken, so the actual hailstone was much bigger. Although lighter than the Coffeyville hailstone it is recognised by the National Climate Extremes Committee, the body responsible for validating records, as the biggest hailstone in the United States. It is preserved in the deep freeze at the National Center for Atmospheric Research, Boulder, Colorado.*

Hail speed

The speed with which a hailstone falls depends on its size. One researcher came up with the suggestion that the terminal velocity (the speed at which it hits the ground) is 'roughly proportional to the square root of its diameter'. This means a 1 cm (0.39 inch) hailstone ploughs into the ground at 50 km/h (31 mph). The giant Coffeyville 144 mm (5.67 inch) hailstone, one of the largest known, is thought to have fallen at a speed of 169 km/h (105 mph).

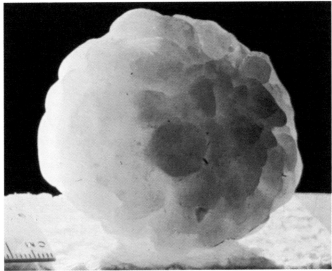

ABOVE A massive hailstone, 7.5 cm (3 inches) in diameter; shown here at actual size.

FACT
The most notorious region for large hailstones is northern India and Bangladesh, where more hail-related deaths are recorded than anywhere else in the world. China is also known for its killer hail storms.

Unusual hail

Hail comes in all shapes and sizes, and since the nineteenth century reports of odd-shaped hailstones have regularly emerged:

22 August 1893: *A hailstorm on the Lincolnshire Wolds, England, flattened cereal crops and gardens, smashed glass, beat chickens to death and caused a horse to bolt and a dog to be killed. The hailstones were not smooth and round but irregular shapes with sharp spikes of ice sticking out, like stars.*

10 August 1898: *Prince William County, Virginia, United States, was the location for another strange hailstorm. The hailstones were flat plates of ice, up to 51 mm (2 inches) long and 19 mm (0.75 inches) thick. Similar hailstones fell in Portland, Oregon, in 1894.*

7 April 1962: *The SS Afghanistan was at anchor off Umm Said, Qatar, when it was hit by hail the size of tennis balls. Some hailstones were even bigger, at least 127 mm (5 inches) in diameter. The sea was a 'mass of white foam' caused by splashes from the hail, and the ship's brass covers for its compasses were badly dented.*

ABOVE This Boeing 737 was struck by heavy hail during a commercial flight over Europe.

Turtle hail
On the afternoon of Friday 11 May 1894, a hailstorm at Bovina, 13 km (8 miles) east of Vicksburg, Mississippi, delivered a hailstone complete with an 20-cm (8-inch) long gopher turtle inside! It must have been sucked up by a waterspout.

Exploding hail
On 11 November 1911, large hailstones, each about 25 mm (1 inch) long and weighing 225 g (8 ounces), came down in a hailstorm in Virginia, United States, and exploded when they hit the ground like popping popcorn. The sound was so loud it could have been mistaken for breaking windowpanes or pistol shots.

Floating hail
A hailstorm at Baghdad and Hinaida, Iraq, on 24 April 1930 was unusual in that the hailstones almost 'floated' to the ground. They were over 25 mm (1 inch) in diameter and would have been expected to hit the ground at more than 48 km/h (30 mph), but their descent was timed against the wall of a building and found to be little more than 15 km/h (9 mph), indicating an upward current of air of at least 48 km/h (30 mph) blowing unusually close to the ground.

Hail or ice block?
A letter in *Scientific American* (1882) described how a gang of railway workers near Salina, Kansas, ran for their lives when hailstones weighing up to 2.3 kg (5 pounds) came raining down. One piece they picked up was estimated to be 36 kg (80 pounds). It was placed in sawdust to stop it melting, and by evening it was 74 cm (29 inches) long, 41 cm (16 inches) wide and 50 mm (2 inches) thick. There was also a cigar-shaped hailstone over 30 cm (1 foot) long and 10 cm (4 inches) in diameter.

Ice blocks from the sky

Large hailstones are one thing, but throughout history there have been reports of large blocks of ice dropping mysteriously from the sky. Theories put forward to explain this phenomenon include ice falling from the wings of airplanes, violent or unusual weather patterns or small comets (which are made of ice and dust) entering the Earth's atmosphere and striking the ground, but no one explanation has yet been proved to be correct.

Late 1700s: *Reports came out of India describing a block of ice 'as big as an elephant' dropping from the sky and taking three days to melt.*

December 1950: *A man driving to Dumbarton, Scotland was almost struck by a rain of ice blocks. The police collected and weighed the fragments and they totalled 50 kg (112 pounds).*

1951: *A carpenter, working on a roof in Kempton, Germany, was killed by a 1.8-m (6-foot) long shaft of ice.*

1957: *A farmer in Bernville, Pennsylvania, United States was narrowly missed not by one but by two spheres of ice, one weighing about 23 kg (50 pounds).*

1965: *The roof of the Phillips Petroleum Plant in Woods Cross, Utah, United States, was punctured by a 23-kg (50-pound) block of ice.*

1973: *The best-documented icefall occurred in Manchester, England. British meteorologist R. F. Griffiths was waiting at a street corner when a huge chunk of ice fell from the sky and smashed into the road just 3 m (10 feet) from where he was standing. The largest piece he recovered weighed 1.6 kg (3 pounds).*

January 16 2000: *Reports emerged from Spain of large blocks of ice, about the size of basketballs, dropping from clear skies. Aircraft waste was eliminated as an explanation as the ice was clear and consisted of pure water.*

Snow

Snow is a form of precipitation consisting not of water droplets but of individually formed ice crystals. It is created when water vapour condenses high in the atmosphere, where the air temperature is below freezing at 0°C (32°F).

Ice nuclei

Snow differs from rain in that the properties of particles acting as ice nuclei are very precise. Sea salt, for example, fails to make good ice nuclei, whereas clays, such as kaolinite and illite, do. About 85 per cent of ice crystals analysed in Greenland have a clay particle at their centre. Decomposing leaf matter is also good for ice nuclei.

Snow crystal types

All snow crystals have six-sided symmetry. It is often said that no two snowflakes are alike, but this, of course, would be impossible to verify. Basic shapes include:

Capped column: *Resembles a cotton reel*
Stellar: *Star-like with six sides but unstable*
Plate: *Flat hexagonal plate*
Column: *Resembling a Greek or Gothic column or bullet-shaped*
Needle: *Miniature bamboo sticks associated with heavy snowfalls*

FACT
While the Chinese were intrigued by the shape of snow crystals as early as 200 BCE, it was not until 1611, that German astronomer Johannes Kepler (1571–1630) published what is thought to be the first scientific description of snow crystals in a pamphlet called *On the Six-Cornered Snowflake.*

FACT
If snowflakes fall at a rate of 3.6–6.4 km/h (2–4 mph), it could take about an hour for one to fall from a cloud to the ground.

World snow

There is less chance of snow falling at or near sea level at latitudes close to the Equator, the delineation generally accepted as 35° North and 40° South. Even in the bitterly cold Polar Regions, very little snow falls each year because at polar temperatures the air mass loses its ability to hold water vapour. Ironically, permanent snow can be present at or near the Equator, for the higher the altitude the greater the prospect of snow. Therefore, snow is present on East Africa's Mount Kilimanjaro, for example, but the only snow actually on the Equator is at 4,690 m (15,390 feet) on the southern slopes of Volcán Cayambe in the Andes of Ecuador, South America.

Throughout the world, 65 countries have snowfalls at sea level to 1,000 m (3,280 feet), and a further 35 have snow at higher altitudes.

Giant snow drift

The greatest accumulation of snow during a winter season occurred on Mount Baker, Washington State. During the winter of 1998–99, 28.96 m (1,140 feet) of snow piled up on its slopes. The previous record had been held by Mount Rainier, also in Washington State, with 28.5 m (93.5 feet) of snow in the winter of 1971–72.

ABOVE AND RIGHT Images of snowflakes captured by Wilson Bentley in 1902.

Snow terms

Blizzard: *A storm with high winds and a heavy fall of snow.*

Bluffart: *Scottish name for a sharp squall with a short snowfall.*

Flurries: *Periods of light snowfall that tend not to settle on the ground.*

Ground blizzard: *Strong winds drive fallen snow into drifts and whiteouts.*

Packing snow: *Snow near melting point that is great for snowball fights and building snowmen.*

Slush: *Snow that is melting into puddles with ice floating in them.*

Snizzle: *Frozen drizzle, a light fall of very small snowflakes or ice particles.*

Snow squall: *A short but intense storm with a heavy fall of snow.*

Snowstorm: *A storm that lasts for a long time accompanied by heavy snowfall.*

Siberian Express

The 'Siberian Express' or 'Alberta Clipper' is an extremely cold flow of air that originates in Siberia, moves across to Alaska and northern Canada before heading south into the United States.

Blizzards

A snowstorm becomes a blizzard when the winds blow at 56 km/h (35 mph) or more, air temperature drops to -7°C (19°F) or below, and falling snow restricts visibility to 150 m (500 feet) or less. In the United States, blizzards are common in the northern Great Plains states. South Dakota, for example, is sometimes known as the 'blizzard state'.

Great white hurricane

The 'Blizzard of 1888' was the worst in American history. It occurred between 11 and 14 March, bringing the east coast from Chesapeake Bay to Maine to an abrupt halt. Major cities, such as New York, Boston, Philadelphia and Washington, DC lost contact with the outside world when telegraph and telephone cables were brought down. Emergency services were put out of action and over 400 people died.

The storm was preceded by several days of unusually mild weather, but rain turned to heavy snow when the air temperature plummeted. During the next 36 hours, 127 cm (50 inches) of snow was dumped on the states of Massachusetts and Connecticut and 102 cm (40 inches) buried New York and New Jersey. Winds piled the snow into drifts 12–15 m (40–50 feet) high.

Black snow

On 30 January 1897, black snow fell on Eskdalemuir, Scotland. The surface of unbroken snow was blackened to a depth of 6 mm (0.25 inches), yet the snow below was the usual white. A 6.4-km (4-mile) stretch of countryside was blanketed in the black snow, although it was not even. The cause of the black snow was probably soot from a nearby manufacturing town.

ABOVE A college hiking group struggles through blizzard conditions on Mt Washington, New Hampshire, United States.

Giant snowflakes

From time to time in recent history, there are records of snowflakes of exceptional size. On 7 January 1887, for example, snowflakes up to 100 mm (4 inches) in diameter and 40 mm (1.6 inches) thick fell at Chepstow, England. The large flakes were composed of hundreds of undamaged crystals joined together. Even larger flakes fell at Fort Keogh, Montana, United States, on 28 January in the same year. They measured 38 cm (15 inches) across by 20 cm (8 inches) thick.

Antarctic in the United States

The weather around Mount Washington in the state of New Hampshire, United States is sometimes as harsh as that of the Antarctic. Wind chills have been reported to drop the temperature to -84°C (-119°F), and the strongest wind speed ever recorded on the planet – a speed of 372 km/h (231 mph) – was experienced here, where the average wind speed is gale force and every third day it is hurricane-force. The annual average air temperature is about -3°C (26.6°F), the lowest measured at -44°C (-47°F). An average of 6.5 m (21.3 feet) of snow falls each year, with maximum falls of up to 14.3 m (47 feet). Buildings near the summit, known as the 'City in the Clouds', are often covered with rime ice, resembling 'sideways icicles', which forms in the thick fogs that envelop the mountain for 60 per cent of the year.

FACT

Snow falling from a cloudless sky is a phenomenon sometimes seen in severe cold and calm air conditions in polar regions. The snow can be different shapes, ranging from ice needles to star shapes to flat snowflakes and ice granules without structure. The snow sparkles in the sunlight and has become known by polar explorers as 'diamond dust'.

Ice Age

Between three million and ten thousand years ago, much of the world was enveloped by ice and snow. This was the time of the last Great Ice Age, which started about 45 million years ago, and which technically we are still experiencing. It was not an era of continuous cold, but long icy periods separated by shorter interludes of almost tropical conditions. Mountain glaciers formed on all the continents, and an ice sheet several thousand feet thick covered parts of North America and Eurasia.

Little Ice Age

This was a period of cooling temperatures recorded from the fourteenth to mid-nineteenth centuries. It included cold spells starting in 1650, 1770 and 1850, separated by warmer intervals. Pack ice moved further south in the Atlantic, with records of Eskimos landing in Scotland. Swiss glaciers advanced, engulfing villages and farms. The River Thames in London, England, and Dutch rivers and canals froze over, and folk there held 'ice fairs'. New York Harbour froze during the winter of 1780 and people could walk from Manhattan to Staten Island. Iceland was ice-bound and European colonies in Greenland died out. Springs and summers were cold and wet and disrupted agriculture gave rise to widespread food shortages.

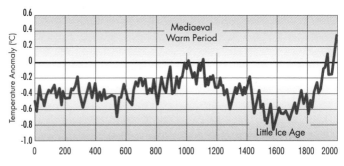

ABOVE A scientific reconstruction of the Earth's surface temperature over the last 2000 years, showing how much it varied from current average global temperatures.

WIND
AND STORMS

What is wind?

Uneven heating of the Earth's surface causes air to move mainly horizontally between air masses, causing 'wind.' Wind flows between air masses of different barometric pressure, from high pressure to low pressure, in an attempt to even them out. Winds can be local breezes caused by temperature differences between land and sea, or be global winds caused by an enormous differentiation between the temperatures at the Equator and the Poles.

Prevailing winds

If our planet did not rotate, there would be a simple flow of warm air from the Equator to the Poles in the upper atmosphere, because hot air rises, and a flow of cooler air from the Poles to the Equator nearer the ground, because cool air falls. However, the Earth does rotate, with the result that this simple pattern is made much more complex. Across the world, there are bands of winds that blow in different directions depending on the latitude; these winds have been familiar to sailors for centuries and have well-established names.

Trade winds

These are the most reliable winds on the planet, winds on which mariners in sailing ships relied to carry them from Europe to the Americas. They form under what is known as the 'Hadley Cell' on either side of the Equator. This meteorological phenomenon carries warm air upward at the Equator and transports it toward the Poles. At latitudes 30° North and South the air cools and descends, making its way back to the Equator, albeit with a shift to the west due to the Coriolis effect (a force associated with the rotation of the Earth). In the Northern Hemisphere the winds blow from the northeast and are known as the Northeast Trades. In the Southern Hemisphere they blow from the southeast and are the Southeast Trades. The name 'trade' comes from the Old English word *trade* meaning 'track', giving rise to the expression 'the wind blows trade' or 'on track'.

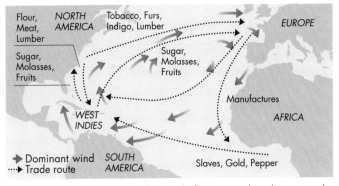

Flour,
Meat,
Lumber · NORTH AMERICA
Tobacco, Furs,
Indigo, Lumber · EUROPE
Sugar,
Molasses,
Fruits
Sugar,
Molasses,
Fruits
Manufactures · AFRICA
WEST INDIES
→ Dominant wind
⋯→ Trade route · SOUTH AMERICA
Slaves, Gold, Pepper

ABOVE Prevailing Atlantic winds had a crucial influence on eighteenth-century trade.

Roaring forties

The name 'roaring forties' was applied by mariners to strong and steady westerlies occurring between latitudes 40° and 50° South, where they are unhindered by major land masses.

Polar easterlies

A permanent body of falling cold air dominates the high latitude end of the 'Polar Circulation Cell', and winds caused by the outflow of air from that cell are cool, strong and unrelenting. They blow in both hemispheres. In the Northern Hemisphere, they sometimes combine with warm moist air from the Gulf Stream, producing violent thunderstorms and even tornadoes, such as the devastating 1987 Edmonton tornado, as far north as latitude 60° on the North American continent.

Westerlies

These winds are linked to a mid-latitude phenomenon known as the 'Ferrel Cell'. This cell balances the Hadley and Polar Circulation Cells and its air moves in the same direction as our planetary rotation. Eddy currents are created that cause the airflow and, therefore, the wind at the Earth's surface to flow mainly from west to east.

Jet streams

These are upper level winds that move generally eastward in the tropopause (the continuously moving boundary between the troposphere and stratosphere) at the junction between the Polar Circulation Cell and Ferrel Cell. They also form in winter at latitudes of 30° at the junction between Hadley and Ferrel cells. Jet streams are not continuous around the world and their tracks can shift to north and south.

Doldrums

These are an area of calm close to the Equator, between latitudes 5° North and South, where the air rises but does not blow horizontally. Sailors caught here found the weather conditions depressing so it became known as the 'doldrums'. The area is known technically as the 'Intertropical Convergence Zone' or ITCZ. The trade winds converge here and produce some of the world's heaviest rainfalls.

Horse latitudes

This is a name given to a band between 30° and 35° North and 30° and 35° South – the boundary between the Hadley and Ferrel cells. Here, dry air descends, high pressure dominates and winds are weak. It is also known as the subtropical high. According to folklore, sailors gave the region this name because their sailing ships were stranded and they threw any livestock, such as horses, overboard in an attempt to save on provisions.

FACT

A 'microburst' wind was responsible for the crash of a commercial airliner at Dallas-Fort Worth International Airport in 1985.

Microbursts and macrobursts

Tornadoes are often blamed for damage caused by 'microbursts'. These are winds that blast down to the ground from thunderstorms at speeds of more than 240 km/h (150 mph), destroying buildings, blowing down trees and probably accounting for some aircraft crashes. The phenomenon is known generally as a 'downburst', but if it affects an area less than 4 km (2.5 miles) square it is known as a 'microburst', and if it affects a larger area it is a 'macroburst'.

Mesoscale winds

These are winds that rise and fall in a short time and generate their own weather. Many have local names, as seen below:

Country	Local names for mesoscale winds
Argentina	Pampero, Suestado, Williwaw, Zonda
Australia	Brickfielder, Cockeyed Bob, Fremantle Doctor, Guba
Canada/ Northern USA	Barber, Chinook, Nor'easter, Piterak, Squamish, Taku, Knik
Central America	Chubasco, Papagayo
France	Aspre, Auster, Autan, Maestro, Marin, Mistral/Cierzo
Greece	Etesian/Meltemi, Euros, Gregale, Lips, Vardar, Zephyr/Zephyros
Hawaii	Kona, Mauka, Pali
India	Bhoot, Elephanta, Brubu
Italy	Bentu de Soli (Sardinia), Libeccio, Sirocco, Garigliano/Tramontana
Mexico	Chocolatero, Cordonazo, Coromell, Nortes, Teheuntepecer
New Zealand	Canterbury Nor'wester
Persian Gulf	Nashi, Shamal, Sharki
Siberia (Russia)	Buran, Burg, Purga
Southwest USA	Blue Norther, Diablo, Haboob, Santa Ana, Sundowner
Switzerland	Bise, Föhn, Maloja
South Africa	Cape Doctor/Black Southeaster, Bull's Eye Squall

Anabatic and katabatic winds

Known also as a valley breeze, an anabatic wind moves up a slope. In
the morning the Sun warms the upper slopes of the mountains while
the valley is in shade. The warm air rises and is replaced by cooler air
from below. Katabatic winds are driven by cold air racing down
slopes, also known as 'mountain breezes'. They can form when cool
air on a cold plateau, such as Mongolia, Antarctica, the Patagonia Ice
Sheet or Greenland, is set in motion under the influence of gravity,
and they can be very fierce.

Windiest place on Earth

The windiest place on Earth close to sea level is Cape Denison in the
Antarctic. It was Australian explorer Douglas Mawson's base in 1911.
On his arrival Mawson found it odd that no sea ice prevented him
from reaching shore, an indication perhaps of strong winds in the
area. Sure enough, the next six months delivered gusts up to 160 km/h
(100 mph), peaking at 320 km/h (200 mph) in May 1912. Mawson
dubbed the Cape and adjacent Commonwealth Bay as 'Home of the
Blizzard'. Its winds are katabatic and are the consequence of the

domed continent and low-
pressure systems at the coast.
Large quantities of icy cold air
slide down the coastal slopes
of the Antarctic ice sheet,
accelerating as they go to
create hurricane force winds
at the edge of the sea.

LEFT Sir Douglas Mawson, British-
Australian explorer, wrapped up
against the Antarctic winds.

Warm Antarctic wind

A 'Föhn bank' is formed by a warm, contour-hugging wind passing over freezing ground. The warm air blowing over the cold land causes ice and snow to change from solid to gas without a liquid phase, a process known as 'sublimation'. The result is a blanket of thick condensed vapour.

Warm katabatic winds

Some katabatic winds form on the lee side – sheltered side – of mountains. As the wind descends, it heats as a consequence of the air mass being compressed. The temperature of the wind can rise by 20°C (36°F) above the surrounding area, and several of the world's locally named winds, such as North America's Chinook, Switzerland's Föhn, France's Mistral and California's Santa Ana, are formed in this way. They are also termed 'orographic winds' in that they are raised up over mountains before descending on the lee side.

Hot winds

During the summer of 1860, the temperature in Alabama, Mississippi, Louisiana and Missouri was hovering around 38°C (100°F) for several days non-stop; but the hottest experience was a searingly hot wind, just 90 m (300 feet) wide, that ploughed across central Georgia scorching cotton crops on a number of plantations. At Kansas, several people were left choking from the fiery blast. The temperature of the wind was reported to be 50°C (122°F).

FACT
On 23 February 1911, a schoolgirl entered an open playground in Bradford, England, in very windy weather. A violent gust picked her up and carried her some 6 m (20 feet) into the air. She then dropped and died on impact with the ground.

Measuring the wind

The oldest weather-measuring device is probably the weathervane, a simple flat object (vane) that swings around to indicate the direction from which the wind is blowing. The vane is often crafted in the shape of an animal, its head pointing into the wind. In Christian countries the most common shape is the cockerel, which started to appear on church roofs, spires and towers in the ninth century, to remind parishioners of the cock that crowed thrice when St. Peter denied three times that he knew Jesus Christ.

Wind speed measurement

The first wind-speed device was a revolving disc anemometer (from the Greek word anemos meaning 'wind') invented by Italian architect Leon Battista Alberti in 1450. Wind is measured today, however, by the spinning cup anemometer, a device with four hemispherical cups attached to a spindle that spins around when blown by the wind.

Wind speed categories

Mariners have always depended on the direction and strength of the wind, but it was not until 1805 that a standard method of wind speed measurement was introduced. Prior to this, although naval officers made regular weather observations, these were very subjective – one man's 'stiff breeze' could easily have been another man's 'calm conditions'. Then, in 1805, Sir Francis Beaufort – an Admiral of the British Navy – introduced a simple scale for recording wind strength at sea. It is known as the Beaufort Scale, or the Beaufort Wind Force Scale. Originally based on the effect the wind had on a ship's sails – from 'just sufficient to give steerage' to 'that which no canvas [sails] could withstand' – in 1906, with the advent of steam power, the descriptions were changed to the effect of the wind on the sea. It was later adapted for use on land. It is divided into 'forces', as listed in the table opposite, with specific signs on land and at sea for each force.

Force	Wind	knots	mph	km/h	Signs at sea	Signs on land
0	Calm	0–1	0–1	0–1	Sea like mirror	Smoke rises vertically
1	Light air	1–3	1–3	1–6	Ripples like scales but no crests	Wind direction shown by wind drift but not wind vanes
2	Light breeze	4–6	4–7	7–11	Short, small wavelets with glassy crests but do not break	Wind on face, vanes move, leaves rustle
3	Gentle breeze	7–10	8–12	12–19	Large wavelets, crests break, glassy foam, scattered white horses (tips)	Leaves and twigs move, flags move
4	Moderate breeze	11–16	13–18	20–29	Small waves become larger, fairly frequent white horses	Raises dust and light litter (paper), small branches move
5	Fresh breeze	17–21	19–24	30–39	Moderate waves, many white horses	Small trees with leaves sway, crested wavelets on inland waters
6	Strong breeze	22–27	25–31	40–50	Large waves forming, extensive white foam crests plus spray	Large branches move, umbrellas put up with difficulty
7	Near gale	28–33	32–38	51–62	Sea heaps up, white foam from breaking waves is streaked in direction of wind	Large trees move, difficulty walking against wind
8	Gale	34–40	39–46	63–75	Moderate high waves with greater length, crests break into spindrift, foam blown in well-marked streaks	Breaks twigs off trees, walking difficult
9	Severe gale	41–47	47–54	76–87	High waves, dense streaks of foam, wave crests topple and roll over	Slight structural damage – chimney tops and roof tiles blown off
10	Storm	48–55	55–63	88–102	Very high waves with long overhanging crests, patches of foam in streaks, sea's surface white, heavy tumbling, visibility reduced	Trees uprooted, greater structural damage
11	Violent storm	56–63	64–72	103–117	Exceptionally high waves hiding ships in trough, sea covered in long white foam patches, edge of wave crests blown into froth, visibility reduced	Widespread damage
12	Hurricane	64–71	73–83	>117	Air filled with foam and spray, sea white with driving spray, visibility seriously reduced.	Mayhem! Violent with serious destruction

(Based on Observers Handbook, Met Office)

Hurricanes, typhoons and cyclones

Hurricanes are probably the most powerful storms on Earth. Exceptionally high winds, incredible rainfall and battering storm surges accompany hurricanes and these can devastate entire coastal areas, destroying everything in their path and killing people living there. It has been estimated that during its life a single hurricane can use as much energy as 10,000 nuclear bombs.

What's in a word?

The word 'hurricane' comes from the Central American god of evil Hurucán (from the Arawak language meaning 'storm') who was familiar to the Taíno tribe of the Greater Antilles in the Caribbean. It is used today to describe tropical storms in the Atlantic and Eastern Pacific. In the western Pacific and China Sea they are known as 'typhoons', from the Cantonese word tai-fung, meaning 'great wind'. Around the Indian subcontinent and Australia they are called 'cyclones', although Australians also adopt the term 'willy-willy'.

ABOVE A satellite image of Hurricane Fran, just before it made landfall on the east coast of the United States in September 1996.

The rise of a hurricane

The hurricane season in the North Atlantic and North Pacific is usually between June and November, and between January and March in the Southern Hemisphere. The most vulnerable areas lie in the ocean between latitudes 8° and 20° North and South. Here, high humidity, light winds and warm sea-surface temperatures are the ingredients that make for a high-intensity tropical storm.

Tropical disturbance: *A hurricane begins to develop when a cluster of thunderstorms, known as a 'tropical disturbance', appear over the tropical ocean. Most North Atlantic hurricanes that hit North America are derived from tropical disturbances that travel from east to west, having originally formed over West Africa.*

Developing force: *Where a hurricane is developing, the air pressure drops when water vapour condenses, releasing latent heat. The warming air rises, expands and then cools, causing more water vapour to condense, and so on until a chain reaction feeds the system and the pressure drops even more. The lower surface pressure encourages additional warm, moist air to flow in, resulting in the formation of more thunderstorms and higher winds. The Coriolis effect causes the winds to rotate in a counterclockwise manner (in the Northern Hemisphere), and they become increasingly strong. The air flowing out the top of the centre of the storm circles down towards the ground forming super-strength winds.*

Tropical storm: *When the persistent wind speed is 37 km/h (23 mph) the tropical disturbance is considered a 'tropical depression', and when the winds blow at 63 km/h (39 mph) it becomes a 'tropical storm'. At this point it is given a name. Tropical storm names were exclusively female until 1953, but since 1979 male and female names alternate. When the wind speed increases to 119 km/h (74 mph) the storm is officially a 'hurricane'.*

Anatomy of a hurricane

The eye: *At the centre of a hurricane is the 'eye'. It resembles a chimney with a diameter of 10–65 km (6–40 miles), and it has no clouds, light winds and sinking air. It is the calmest part of the storm.*

Eye wall: *Surrounding the eye is the 'eye wall'. It is a ring of violent thunderstorms and extremely high winds that deliver a deluge of rain. The highest winds are on the side of the wall that runs parallel to the direction of forward movement of the storm. If the storm is heading due west, for example, the highest winds will be on the northern wall. The result is a combination of the forward motion and the wind itself to create superwinds.*

Spiral centre: *Outside the wall are bands of heavy rain that form in a spiral centred on the eye of the storm – the so-called 'spiralling rain bands'. The strength of wind and rain here can be as half as much as in the eye wall.*

Storm surge

Accompanying the storm can be a rise in sea level of up to 10 m (33 feet), and this dome of water can be 80–160 km (50–100 miles) across. When it sweeps over the coastline, any shoreline structure, such as marinas, piers, docks, oceanside housing developments, bridges, roads and railways, can be seriously damaged or even destroyed by a wall of water.

FACT

The energy in an average hurricane, if harnessed and converted into electricity, could supply power to the entire United States for up to three years.

Saffir-Simpson hurricane scale

The Saffir-Simpson Scale for measuring hurricanes was devised in the 1970s by consultant engineer Herbert Saffir and meteorologist Robert Simpson. It consists of five categories that recognise the press, wind speed and storm surges associated with a hurricane.

Scale	Central air pressure in millibars	Wind speed in kmh (mph)	Storm surge in m (feet)	Damage
1	More than 980	119–153 (74–95)	1.2–1.5 (4–5)	Minimal
2	965–979	154–177 (96–110)	1.8–2.4 (6–8)	Moderate
3	945–964	178–209 (111–130)	2.7–3.7 (9–12)	Extensive
4	920–944	210–249 (131–155)	4–5.5 (13–18)	Extreme
5	Less than 920	More than 249 (155)	More than 5.5 (18)	Catastrophic

Future hurricane names

Names for new hurricanes are determined in advance by the World Meteorological Organisation, using six lists in rotation. If names are not used in one year they are set aside for the list in six years' time. The following name lists have now been issued:

Year	Hurricane name
2006	Alberto, Beryl, Chris, Debby, Ernesto, Florence, Gordon, Helene, Isaac, Joyce, Kirk, Leslie, Michael, Nadine, Oscar, Patty, Rafael, Sandy, Tony, Valerie, William
2007	Andrea, Barry, Chantal, Dean, Erin, Felix, Gabrielle, Humberto, Ingrid, Jerry, Karen, Lorenzo, Melissa, Noel, Olga, Pablo, Rebekah, Sebastien, Tanya, Van, Wendy
2008	Arthur, Bertha, Cristobal, Dolly, Edouard, Fay, Gustav, Hanna, Iko, Josephine, Kyle, Lili, Marco, Nana, Omar, Paloma, Rene, Sally, Teddy, Vicky, Wilfred
2009	Ana, Bill, Claudette, Danny, Erika, Fred, Grace, Henri, Ida, Joaquin, Kate, Larry, Mindy, Nicolas, Odette, Peter, Rose, Sam, Teresa, Victor, Wanda
2010	Alex, Bonnie, Colin, Danielle, Earl, Fiona, Gaston, Hermine, Igor, Julia, Karl, Lisa, Matthew, Nicole, Otto, Paula, Richard, Shary, Tomas, Virginie, Walter

Deadliest Atlantic hurricanes

Great Hurricane

This was the deadliest known hurricane. In October 1780 it ploughed into the Caribbean islands of Martinique, St. Eustatius and Barbados. It was at the time of the American Revolution and it destroyed many ships in the British and French naval fleets that were vying for control of the region. It was one of three powerful hurricanes to hit the area in succession, and it coincided with a record peak in sunspot activity.

Hurricane Mitch

Mitch was one of the most powerful hurricanes ever recorded. Maximum sustained wind speeds of 290 km/h (180 mph) battered Central America in October and November 1998. Most of the damage occurred in Honduras and Nicaragua, where people died in mudslides and flooding.

Galveston Hurricane

On 8 September 1900, an enormous storm surge caused by a hurricane with 200 km/h (125 mph) winds swept over Galveston, Texas, killing more than 8,000 people and destroying 3,636 homes. It was the largest death toll caused by a hurricane in US history.

Season	Hurricane	Human deaths
Oct 1780	Great Hurricane	22,000
1998	Hurricane Mitch	Up to 18,000
Sept 1900	Galveston Hurricane	Up to 12,000
Sept 1974	Hurricane Fifi	Up to 10,000
Sept 1930	Dominican Republic Hurricane	Up to 8,000

Other notable hurricanes

Labor Day Hurricane: *On 2 September 1935, the first category 5 hurricane reported in the United States came ashore at the Florida Keys. Sustained winds were in excess of 250 km/h (155 mph) and gusts reached 338 km/h (210 mph). Of the 423 people killed, 259 were World War I veterans building a bridge from the mainland to the Keys.*

Hurricane Camille: *Camille made landfall at Pass Christian, Mississippi, on 20 August 1969, with sustained winds reaching 305 km/h (190 mph) and gusts over 335 km/h (200 mph). About 256 people were killed and almost 9,000 injured. Damage was not only from the wind, but also from a 7.3 m (24-foot) high storm surge that swept in from the Gulf of Mexico.*

Hurricane Andrew: *Andrew, a category 5 hurricane, first hit the Bahamas on 23 August 1992, then made landfall on the United States at Homestead, Florida, with sustained winds of 265 km/h (165 mph) and gusts of 291 km/h (181 mph). 41 people were killed and over 250,000 people were left homeless. A few days later it moved into the Gulf of Mexico, coming ashore at Burns Point, Louisiana, as a category 3 storm and spawning 47 tornadoes that devastated southern and mid-Atlantic states.*

ABOVE The eye of Hurricane Ivan, the most powerful hurricane of the 2004 Atlantic season. This photograph was taken from on board the International Space Station.

Hurricane Katrina

Hurricane Katrina was the second Category 5 hurricane of the 2005 season, and the sixth strongest ever recorded. The storm formed over the Bahamas on 23 August, but after crossing Florida as a Category 1 hurricane, it gained strength in the Gulf of Mexico. By 28 August, it had increased to Category 5, the air pressure at its centre dropping to 902 millibars and sustained winds reaching 280 km/h (175 mph), making it the strongest hurricane ever recorded in the Gulf.

By its second landfall near Buras-Triumph, Louisiana, on 29 August, and a third on the Louisiana/Mississippi border a few hours later, Katrina had become a Category 3 hurricane, but its vast size meant that it devastated areas over 190 km (120 miles) from its centre with sustained winds of 195-205 km/h (120-125 mph). Levees separating Lake Pontchartrain from New Orleans were breached and 80 per cent of the city was flooded.

Katrina maintained hurricane-strength until close to Jackson, Mississippi, 240 km (150 miles) inland, and downgraded again near Clarksville, Tennessee, where it broke in two. The death toll as of March 2006 is 1,604, with over 2,000 people still unaccounted for.

ABOVE The National Guard patrolling central New Orleans in the aftermath of Hurricane Katrina. At this time much of the city was underwater.

Typhoons

1958 typhoon season

The typhoon season in the Pacific usually lasts from June until December, but in 1958 it ran all year. In January, for example, Typhoon Ophelia's 260 km/h (160 mph) winds devastated Jaluit in the Marshall Islands. In May, following a procession of smaller storms, Super-Typhoon Phyllis had winds peaking at 298 km/h (185 mph), the strongest ever recorded in the region, but it remained over the open sea. In July, Super-Typhoon Winnie blasted through Taiwan and southeast China with 282 km/h (175 mph) winds, while in August the windswept region was host to Typhoon Flossie, which hit Tokyo, with many casualties. In September, Super-Typhoon Helen hit southeast Japan again before heading north, and in the same month Super-Typhoon Ida devastated the Japanese island of Honshu. Over 48,560 hectares (120,000 acres) of rice fields and 2,118 buildings were destroyed with 1,269 casualties.

Windy and wet typhoon

On 28 August 1992, Typhoon Omar slammed into Guam, the strongest since Typhoon Pamela in 1976. Gusts up to 275 km/h (170 mph) and 416.9 mm (16.41 inches) of rain were recorded at Andersen Air Force Base. And on 17 December 1997 events were repeated (but even more so) when Typhoon Paka crossed the island with winds gusting to 381.3 km/h (236.9 mph) and dumping 535 mm (22 inches) of rain before the rain monitoring equipment failed.

FACT
On 15 August 1291, a typhoon moving across the Sea of Japan destroyed an entire Mongol invasion fleet. It became known as the 'Divine Wind' or 'Kamikaze'.

Lowest of the lows

The most intense storm ever recorded was Typhoon Tip, which blew up in the northwest Pacific Ocean on 4 October 1979. Its eye had a minimum pressure at the sea's surface of only 870 millibars – the lowest pressure recorded to date – and maximum sustained winds of 306 km/h (190 mph). It was also the world's largest tropical storm system with a circulation 2,174 km (1,350 miles) across.

Name change ... and back again!

Hurricane John, which formed on 11 August 1994, was the longest-lived tropical storm with a life span of 31 days. During its 13,000 km (8,000 mile) journey around the Pacific, it crossed the international dateline twice and in doing so switched from being Hurricane John to Typhoon John and back again.

Mighty cyclones

On 20 May 1999, *a cyclone with winds in excess of 275 km/h (170 mph) hit the Sindh Province of southern Pakistan. More than 400 people were killed and 600 villages destroyed.*

On 13 November 1970, *a cyclone swept across Bangladesh, pushing a 15 m (50-foot) high storm surge ahead of it. Over 500,000 people were killed and a further 50 million were affected by the storm.*

On 15 December 1999, *Cyclone John ran into the northwest of Australia with winds gusting up to 260 km/h (162 mph). It was the strongest cyclone to hit the island continent in 100 years, but luckily it blew over mostly uninhabited areas. Cyclone Tracey was not so fortunate. It did not measure up to Cyclone John's power, but on 25 December 1974 its 217 km/h (135 mph) winds destroyed much of the city of Darwin and killed 65 people. It was also the world's smallest tropical storm with a circulation just 50 km (30 miles) wide.*

Tornadoes

A tornado starts as a severe thunderstorm known as a 'supercell'. Winds entering the storm begin to swirl and form a tight funnel. The wind in the funnel spins increasingly faster, creating an extremely low pressure that sucks in more air and any object lying in its path. In the United States, the vast, flat Great Plains enable dry polar air from Canada to meet warm moist air from the Gulf of Mexico, so in Oklahoma, Texas, Kansas and Nebraska conditions are ripe for tornadoes to form. It has the highest concentration of tornadoes anywhere in the world, and is a magnet for 'storm chasers'.

Fujita–Pearson Scale for measuring tornadoes

F-no.	Description	Wind speed in km/h (mph)	Damage
F0	Gale tornado	64–116 (40–72)	Chimneys, tree branches broken, shallow rooted trees pushed over
F1	Moderate tornado	118–180 (73–112)	Roof tiles peel, mobile homes pulled off foundations, cars moved
F2	Significant tornado	182–253 (113–157)	Roofs torn off timber houses, mobile homes destroyed, large trees snapped or uprooted, light objects picked up in the air
F3	Severe tornado	254–332 (158–206)	Roofs torn off brick houses, trains overturned, swathes of trees uprooted
F4	Devastating tornado	333–418 (207–260)	Well-constructed houses demolished, cars and other large objects picked up
F5	Incredible tornado	420–512 (261–318)	Timber frame house picked up, car-sized object fly for 100 m (330 feet) or more, steel reinforced concrete buildings damaged
F6	Inconceivable tornado	513–610 (319–379)	Damage extreme and unlikely to be recognisable with the mess produced by F4 and F5 wind that would surround it. The only measurable evidence of this wind existing might be a swirl pattern on the ground.

Killer tornadoes

About 1,000 reported tornadoes track across the United States each year, but year-by-year casualties are falling. Tornadoes causing large numbers of deaths occurred mostly in yesteryear. With better tornado prediction and detection and quicker communications, killer tornadoes are far fewer today.

Killer tornadoes in the United States

F-scale	Date	States and Towns Hit	Dead	Injured
F5	18 March 1925	Missouri/Illinois/Indiana Murphysboro/Gorham/DeSoto	695	2,027
Unknown	7 May 1840	Louisiana/Mississippi Nachez	317	109
F4	27 May 1896	Missouri/Illinois St. Louis/ East St. Louis	255	1,000
F5	5 April 1936	Missouri Tupelo	216	700
F4	6 April 1936	Georgia Gainesville	203	1,600
F5	9 April 1947	Texas/Oklahoma/Kansas Glazier/Higgins/Woodward	181	970
F4	24 April 1908	Louisiana/Missouri Amite/Pine/Purvis	143	770
F5	12 June 1899	Wisconsin New Richmond	117	200
F5	8 June 1953	Missouri Flint	115	844
F5	11 May 1953	Texas Waco	114	597

FACT
The Great Bend tornado that sliced through a part of Kansas in 1915 undoubtedly had the most oddities among its storm debris. Five horses in a barn on a farm at Pawnee Rock were flown, uninjured, a distance of 0.4 km (a quarter of a mile) and were still attached to their rail.

Tornado day
On 3 April 1974, several destructive tornadoes occurred in 11 states and Ontario, Canada, during a single eight-hour period. In Ontario alone nine people were killed and 30 were seriously injured. Damage amounted to $1 billion.

Top wind speed
On 3 May 1999, the University of Oklahoma Doppler-on-Wheels radar unit recorded the wind in an F5 tornado and it was found to be blowing at a speed of 512 km/h (318 mph) about 40 m (130 feet) above the ground. This is the highest natural wind speed recorded to date.

ABOVE Massive tornado damage in Oklahoma, 1973.

French whirlwind

Europe is not often in the news for its devastating tornadoes, but on 19 August 1845 a tornado destroyed homes and mills near Monville, France, killing up to 200 people. It was one of Europe's most devastating tornado disasters.

English tornado

The strongest tornado recorded in Britain struck the suburbs of Birmingham, England, on 28 July 2005. Winds blew up to 210 km/h (130 mph), uprooting trees, picking up cars and injuring people. Surprisingly, Britain has more tornadoes, relative to its land area, than any country in the world.

Dust devils

Not all whirlwinds are large. A letter in the respected journal *Nature* in 1935 describes a dust devil – a rotating column of sand that moves rapidly over open spaces – just 1.5 m (5 feet) high with a column less than 30 cm (12 inches) across that moved along at about 24 km/h (15 mph). The correspondent also recalled a revolving 2.54 cm (1 inch) thick sheet of sand and plant debris just 30 cm (12 inches) high, but with a diameter of 3.7 m (12 feet). It revolved around him for about three minutes, producing a 'swishing sound' before slowly dying away. Locally these miniature dust devils are considered to be spirits, so-called *afrit* or *ginni* (the genie of the *Arabian Nights*).

Steam devil

On 30–31 January 1971, the air temperature barely reached above -21°C (-6°F) off the Milwaukee shoreline of Lake Michigan. Steam fog accumulated over the lake surface, with revolving columns up to 200 m (656 feet) in diameter reaching up over 460 m (1,500 feet) into the cumulus clouds above. The 'steam devils' lasted no longer than a few minutes.

Fiery winds

Flaming cylinder: *On a farm 8 km (5 miles) from Ashland in Cheatham County, Tennessee, in the summer of 1869, a fiery whirlwind scorched everything in its path. The 'flaming cylinder' travelled at about 8 km/h (5 mph), singeing the leaves on trees and burning the manes and tails of horses feeding in a field. Heading towards the farmhouse, it first set a haystack alight and then the shingles, so that after ten minutes the entire building was 'wrapped in flames'. It finally reached a river, where it raised a column of steam that stretched right up to the clouds and then slowly fizzled out. Over 200 people witnessed the extraordinary event.*

Wind fireworks: *In 1881, near Americus, Georgia, a small whirlwind formed over a cornfield. It had a diameter of about 1.5 m (5 feet) and was about 30 m (100 feet) high, but its centre was 'illuminated by fire' and it emitted a 'strange sulphurous vapour'. It occasionally split into three smaller clouds. As the clouds came back together, eyewitnesses heard a loud crash accompanied by cracking sounds, and then the whole thing shot up into the sky.*

ABOVE A dust storm moves across a ploughed field in Arizona.

Dust storms

Between 14 and 24 March 2002, a huge dust storm raged across southern Asia. Driven by high winds, the dust was stirred up in the deserts of Mongolia and northern China, and was then carried across China, Korea and southeast Russia, creating the worst dust storm for 40 years. The dust-laden winds then headed out across the Pacific.

Electrical tornado

On 24 May 1949, a small tornado travelled across a clay tennis court at Curepipe, on the island of Mauritius in the Indian Ocean, and left behind a shallow trench 18 m (60 feet) long, 60 cm (2 feet) wide and up to 100 mm (4 inches) deep. A ball of bright light and a crackling sound like a 'sugar cane fire' accompanied the tornado. Material from the trench, including blocks weighing up to 0.5 kg (1 pound) each, was carried to a distance of 15 m (50 feet). An umpire's chair weighing 23 kg (50 pounds) was carried 18 m (60 feet) into the air. What caused the scorching remains a mystery.

Inside tornadoes

Several eyewitnesses have observed the inside of tornado funnels and lived to tell their tale. They describe a light show of electrical phenomena, such as continuous lightning, brightly shining luminous clouds, great balls of fire and even a display 'like a Fourth of July pinwheel'. 'St. Elmo's fire' (electrical activity in the atmosphere) has been observed near the funnel mouth, along with buzzes and hissings indicative of electrical activity. The smell of ozone and nitrous oxides often pervades the air.

FACT
On 12 May 1934, a black blizzard containing topsoil from the 'Dust Bowl' dumped 12 million tons of dust on Chicago.

THUNDER
AND LIGHTNING

The power of gods

Such is the power locked up in a thunderstorm that it was once thought of as the ultimate weapon by our ancestors. Thor, the Norse god of thunder, wielded a large and heavy hammer, which delivered the thunderbolts that fell from the sky. In general, however, a god of thunder was worshipped wherever people regularly experienced heavy thunderstorms or thunder preceded the arrival of life-giving rains after prolonged periods of drought.

What is thunder?

The sound that so impressed the ancients was nothing more than the shockwave caused when lightning heats the air around it to a temperature exceeding 30,000°C (54,000°F) – many times hotter than the surface of the Sun. The superheated air expands and then almost as quickly contracts. This rapid but brief period of expansion and contraction generates a sound wave that we hear as 'thunder'.

Thunderstorm formation

For a thunderstorm to develop, three elements must be present – warm air, moisture and an unstable air mass. The warm air rises, either when the Sun heats the ground, when a front passes and the air is pushed aloft or when the air mass moves up the side of a mountain. The rising moist air reaches a height where it cools and water vapour condenses to form cotton-wool-like cumulus clouds. During the condensation process, latent heat is released, warming more air and feeding the process. The updraught brings in even more warm moist air causing the towering cloud – probably a dark cumulonimbus by now – to grow up through the atmosphere, even into the stratosphere 16 km (10 miles) above the ground. The extraordinary updraughts in a severe thunderstorm can exceed 160 km/h (100 mph). As precipitation falls, it cools the air forming downdraughts. A mature thunderstorm then has updraughts and downdraughts that stir up the air mass and make the storm even stronger.

ABOVE A thunder cloud is extremely dark because of its density of moisture.

How far away?

You can work out very roughly the distance of an approaching or receding thunderstorm by counting the number of seconds between the flash of the lightning and the sound of the thunderclap. This is because light travels at 299,792.458 km/sec (186,282.397 mps) and sound at 1,225 km/h (761 mph), so the light arrives at the place where you are much faster than the sound. It is said that the storm is about one mile away for every five seconds interval (one kilometre away for every three seconds interval). If the flash and thunderclap occur at the same time, the storm is directly overhead.

Windsheer

The updraughts and downdraughts inside a cumulonimbus thundercloud are so violent that changes of direction of the air mass can occur over relatively short distances, both vertically and horizontally. Windsheer is of great concern to aircraft pilots. When an aircraft is landing and relying on the uplift of the headwind to keep it aloft, a sudden change of direction downward – a microburst or downburst – will cause it to plough into the ground.

Lightning formation

Inside a storm cloud are rapidly moving masses of air, filled with water and ice. The updraughts and downdraughts sweep the ice particles up and down, each gathering increasingly more layers of ice, like an onion, to form hail, but both the water droplets and hail pellets are torn asunder and smashed together so violently by the ferocious air movements that they are charged with static electricity. Very light, positively charged particles of ice and water tend to accumulate at the top of the cloud, while those with negative charge are at the base. The difference between the charges eventually becomes so great that they neutralise within the cloud with a violent flash of lightning, so-called 'sheet lightning' or 'intracloud lightning'. Charges can travel between clouds too, creating 'spider lightning' that can travel across the sky for up to 145 km (90 miles). However, the ground is also positively charged, so when a cloud is very tall, the shorter route for the lightning to take is not to the top of the cloud but to the ground, producing 'forked' or 'cloud-to-ground' lightning.

FACT
Lightning strikes somewhere on the surface of the Earth about 100 times every second, and at any moment 1,800 thunderstorms occur somewhere on the planet.

Electrifying

Benjamin Franklin nearly lost his life when he tried to understand the nature of lightning. In 1752, he and his son William flew a homemade silk kite in a thunderstorm in Philadelphia, Pennsylvania. Franklin senior was holding the line when lightning struck the kite. Electricity travelled down the wire and sparks jumped from a key that was attached. Fortunately, he was none the worse for his experience and went on to describe that lightning is electricity.

Over in a flash

A bolt of lightning lasts for about 0.2 seconds. It starts when a 'stepped leader' zigzags down from the cloud. Each step is about 45 m (150 feet) long, so when the leader is within 45 m (150 feet) of a positively charged object, such as a flagpole, tree, church spire or any object sticking out above its surroundings, a surge of electricity known as a 'streamer' rises up to meet it. Leader and streamer then form a channel, and the current rising rapidly up the channel causes a flash, known as a 'down stroke'. The bolt itself is no wider than a coin, but appears wider because of the brightness.

ABOVE Multiple cloud-to-ground lightning bolts captured by time-lapse photography.

Lightning hot spots in the United States

The occurrence of lightning is by no means universal. In the United States, central Florida has the most air-to-ground lightning strikes, while the Pacific Northwest and Hawaii have almost none. Across the country, as many as 10,000 forest fires are triggered by lightning and, since 1940, lightning has killed 8,316 people. Despite the success of weather forecasting and the forewarning of dangerous thunderstorms, 363 people are struck in the United States each year and there are 80–90 deaths. The most dangerous month is July, and 7.30 PM is five times more dangerous than 9 AM.

Lightning never strikes twice... or does it?

On 3 January 2001, a gang of 213 inmates was walking back to the prison buildings at Kabwe, Zambia, when they were caught in a severe thunderstorm. The first bolt of lightning hit a group of 20 men, who fell to the ground, and this was closely followed by a second strike on another group. Three prisoners were burned to death, and 17 others received less serious injuries.

Who is at risk?

Covering 35 years of statistics, a 1979 study of lightning strikes in the United States found that walkers in the open and people, including children, in parks and playgrounds were the most at risk.

Activity	Percentage deaths
Open field, park, playground	26.8
Under trees	13.7
Water-related activities, such as boating and swimming	8.1
Golf courses	4.9
Driving tractors, farm and heavy road equipment	3
On telephones	2.4
Near radios, transmitters, aerials	0.7
Other activities or unknown	40

Lightning course

A golf course is one of the worst places to be in a thunderstorm, as the highest object around is often you. Golfing legend Lee Trevino knows from painful experience. On 27 June 1975 during the Western Open, near Chicago, a lightning bolt hit a lake nearby and 'bounced', hitting both Trevino and another player. They were both treated for burns and Trevino was also operated on for a back injury that permanently damaged the flexibility of his spine. He adjusted to the problem, however, and went on to win many more tournaments.

Channeling lightning

Benjamin Franklin developed the lightning conductor, an invention that for philanthropic reasons he did not patent. It consists simply of a pointed rod that projects above a building, such as the top of a church spire, and is joined to a large metal plate buried in the ground by a copper strip. The lightning hits the rod, travels down the strip and is earthed to the ground. The copper strip can vapourise but the building will be relatively safe. In this way a building is afforded some protection against lightning strikes.

Offer prayers

Prior to Franklin's important discoveries about lightning and its nature, Christian churches throughout Europe were prone to lightning strikes – after all, they were the tallest buildings around. Priests attempted to limit damage by saying prayers, sanctifying bells and burning witches. The sound of the bells was to 'temper the destruction of hail and cyclones and the force of tempests and lightning; check hostile thunders and great winds; and cast down the spirits of storms and the powers of the air.' However, it was probably the bell ringers who needed the help not the buildings for they were frequently electrocuted or burned. In 1745, it led author Peter Ahlwardts, who wrote *Reasonable and Theological Considerations about Thunder and Lightning*, to suggest that the last place anyone would want to seek sanctuary during a thunderstorm was a church!

FACT
Thunder can be heard about 19 km (12 miles) away at most, even when things generally are quiet, but lightning can be seen at night up to 160 km (100 miles) away. The average lighting bolt is about 4.8 km (3 miles) long and carries a current of 100 million volts at 10,000 amps.

Ball lightning

This is a rare phenomenon that can appear after a bolt of forked lightning has struck the ground. It creates a violet, red, orange or yellow brightly glowing ball, which can be as small as a tennis ball or as large as a basketball, and it appears to 'float' aimlessly above the ground. It lasts for no more than a few seconds before spluttering out or disappearing with an unexpected bang. Ball lightning is generally described as spherical, but dumbbell, rod and torpedo shapes have been known.

Kitchen incident

On 8 August 1976, according to a letter in the journal *Nature*, a number of houses around Smethwick, in the Midlands, England, were struck by lightning. In one house, a woman was in her kitchen when a 10-cm (4-inch) diameter sphere of bright blue to purple light surrounded by a flame-coloured halo appeared over her stove. The ball moved toward her, about 95 cm (3 feet) above the floor. She felt heat, smelled burning and heard a rattling sound. As it hit her, she brushed it away and it exploded with a bang and vanished. Her hand was red and swollen and her gold wedding ring felt as if it was burning her finger. At the point of impact there was a hole in her dress and her legs were red and numb, but not burned. The synthetic material of the dress was shrivelled around the hole but not charred.

Garden incident

On 10 November 1940, Mr E. Mats was working in his garden in Coventry, England, when suddenly he was surrounded by blackness. When he looked down he saw a pale blue-green fireball about 60 cm (2 feet) across and made of what appeared to be 'writhing strings of lights'. It rose and moved away, just missing a poplar tree. It cleared a neighbouring house by about 6 m (20 feet) and descended about 0.4 km (0.25 miles) away, where it exploded.

Flyswatter incident

On 25 August 1965, Mr and Mrs Greenlee and a neighbour were sitting on their fibreglass-screened, roofed patio, in Dunnellon, Florida. Mrs. Greenlee had just swatted a fly, when suddenly a ball of lightning with the appearance of the flash seen in arc welding appeared in front of her. The flyswatter 'edged in fire' fell to the floor and the ball exploded with a report 'like a shotgun blast'. Nobody was hurt and there were no marks on the patio floor. Turning to Mrs Greenlee, the neighbour said 'You sure got him that time!'

Mile high incident

On 19 March 1963, Eastern Airlines flight 539 from New York to Washington flew into an electrical storm and was 'enveloped in a sudden bright and loud electrical discharge'. A few seconds later a glowing sphere about 20 cm (8 inches) in diameter came out of the flight deck and passed down the aisle at waist height. It was blue-white in colour and glowed like a 5–10-watt light bulb.

ABOVE Cloud-to-ground lightning during a night-time thunderstorm.

FACT
Lightning generates radio waves, ranging in frequency from audible 3 KHz (very low frequency) to 10 MHz (shortwave radio). The low-frequency waves can travel all the way around the world, whereas the shortwave signatures can only make it halfway, and on the side of the Earth that is dark. These higher frequency waves can be heard as a myriad of tiny bells ringing at the same time.

Natural fireworks

On 22 July 1926, a group of academics observed very unusual lightning in the sky above Calcutta, India. There were some misty clouds but the stars were visible, and they saw flashes every minute or so from the lower clouds. Every three minutes, however, there were a series of vivid bursts coloured blue or yellow, followed by luminous trails, like purple ribbons, that shot up at an angle into the sky and exploded like fireworks…they were not fireworks for the flashes were too high and no thunder was heard. Similar lightning trails emanating from the tops of cumulus clouds and shooting up into the sky were seen by crews of the MV *Geesthaven* in the North Atlantic in October 1967, the TSS *British Bombardier* off southern Italy in March 1971, a Royal Australian Air Force aircraft at Broome, Australia in February 1945 and by an observer in Fiji in June 1950. The cause is a mystery.

Red Sprites

Newly discovered 'Red Sprites' jump the 65 km (40-mile) gap between the tops of thunderstorms and the lower ionosphere. They resemble red-coloured jellyfish with blue tentacles. They produce powerful radio emissions and atmospheric gamma ray bursts.

Crawlers and giants

Lightning that spreads across a squall line or frontal system is known as 'lightning crawler' or 'spider'. Radar has detected crawlers at high altitudes – up to 6,100 m (20,000 feet). They can travel horizontally as much as 120 km (75 miles), hopping from one cloud to the next. If they should finally strike the ground, it can be extremely dangerous. Such a strike is known as a 'positive giant' or 'bolt from the blue'. The strike travels from the top of the thundercloud's 'anvil' down to the ground, carrying more destructive energy than a normal lightning strike. It also means lightning can appear out of a cloudless sky.

Old crawlers

On 16 July 1873, there was an extraordinary flash of lightning at Hereford, England. The storm was some 8 km (5 miles) away, but a bolt of lightning raced across the sky, missing narrowly two church spires, but singling out a small house much lower than those surrounding it. The same phenomenon was experienced near Bloomington, Indiana, on 23 July 1926, when a storm about 5 km (3 miles) away released a bolt of lightning that appeared to the local people to come out of a clear blue sky. The stroke, according to eyewitnesses, missed several buildings and hit a small house. Two children were killed. In those days, nobody knew the cause, but today we can identify those strikes as powerful positive giants.

Photographic lightning

Benjamin Franklin described the first authenticated case of photographic lightning at the French Academy in 1786. He described how a man standing opposite a tree struck by lightning later found a facsimile of the tree on his chest. Similarly, in 1853 the *New York Journal of Commerce* described how a young girl was standing at an open window near a maple tree. After a flash of lightning, an image of the tree was found imprinted on her body.

Which trees are vulnerable?

In 1907, the UK's Royal Meteorological Society published the results of a study in the forests of Lippi-Detmold from 1874 to 1890 in which a Dr Hess recorded the types of tree most struck by lightning. The forest consisted of 11 per cent oak, 70 per cent beech, 13 per cent spruce, 6 per cent Scots pine and a handful of other tree types, but it was not the beech trees that were hit most often.

The study showed that all trees are liable to be struck by lightning, but that oak trees and other species with deep roots were most often struck. It went on to speculate that the deep roots made better conductors to the moist subsoil.

ABOVE Dr Hess found that the oak tree is far more likely to be struck by lightning than any other species.

LIFE, LANDSCAPES AND WEATHER

Animal forecasters

Sharks have a sixth electrical sense and birds can detect the Earth's magnetic field, but generally animals have the same basic senses that we do. The difference is that they are able to recognise things to which we are 'blind'. Unlike humankind, protected from nature in our modern, centrally heated 'caves', animals must be in tune with their environment; their very survival depends on being aware of the weather, and possibly even being able to predict it, at least in the short term.

Punxsutawney Phil

'Punxsutawney Phil' from Pennsylvania is the world's most famous weather forecaster. He is not human: he is a groundhog. It is said that if the rodent emerges from his burrow at Gobbler's Knob on 2 February, known as Groundhog Day, and he can see his shadow, winter will last for six more weeks. To date, he has seen his shadow six years in succession. The tradition has its roots in a Christian festival – Candlemass Day, which commemorates the time when the Virgin Mary went to Jerusalem to be purified 40 days after the birth of her son. The prediction is taken from old European sayings. In Scotland, the rhyme is 'if Candlemass day is bright and clear, there'll be two winters in the year', and in England it is 'if Candlemass be fair and bright, winter has another fight; if Candlemass brings cloud and rain, winter will not come again'.

Cat fur

It is said that if cats lick themselves the weather is likely to be fair, and there is a grain of truth in this. If relative humidity is low during good weather, especially in winter, static electricity can build up in a cat's fur as the animal brushes past objects in the home. When it licks itself, it moistens the fur so the charge cannot build. This gave rise to the expression: 'if a cat washes her face o'er her ear, 'tis a sign the weather will be fine and clear'.

Grounded

Birds are genetically programmed to be able to appreciate changes in barometric pressure and react, for instance, to an approaching low-pressure system by reducing their activity. Birds tend to roost more often and longer in low pressure than in high pressure. Many simply sit out a storm and prior to a hurricane huge flocks of seabirds can be seen roosting. The lower air density in a low-pressure system would make flying more difficult, of course, but also the lack of updraughts, associated with warm weather, would discourage larger birds from flying. This gives some credibility to the adage, 'seagull, seagull, sit on the sand; it's a sign of rain when you are at hand'.

All-weather cow

Cattle seem to know their weather. In Europe, cattle appear to stand in good weather but lie down when bad weather is approaching. If half are standing and half lying, then it is 'showery', or so the farmers will tell you. Cows also stand with their tail into the wind. In this way, they can see danger in front and smell when a predator is approaching from behind. In New England, this behavior has given rise to the weather saying 'a cow with its tail to the west, makes weather the best; a cow with its tail to the east, makes weather least'. On the east coast of North America this makes some sense, because more often than not an east wind off the Atlantic Ocean carries rain, and a west wind over the continent is dry.

FACT
Birds that catch insects on the wing, such as swallows, swifts and martins, follow the 'aerial plankton' of tiny flying insects that are swept aloft by columns of warm air rising from the ground. Insects fly closer to the ground in bad weather, so the birds will fly lower down too.

LEFT The great green bush cricket makes one of the loudest chirping sounds among all crickets and is also one of the largest insects living in northern Europe.

Insect thermometer

Crickets are considered useful thermometers. During the mating season, male crickets 'chirp' by rubbing their wings together, and when it is warm they increase the speed of this chirping. Conversely, if it is cold they slow down. There is, indeed, a simple formula based on a cricket's chirps that will give the actual air temperature. Count the number of chirps for 15 seconds, add 40, and you have the approximate temperature in Fahrenheit.

Biting flies

Flies bite more frequently before rain. Flying uses more energy when the air is moist, so flying insects will touch down on anything, including you. You are likely to attract them when a low-pressure system is moving in because you tend to release more body odours. And if a biting fly lands on you, it usually bites.

Ant storm

A sure sign that thunderstorms are looming is when garden ants swarm in summer. In Britain, July is the month when queens and males rise up on thermals – warm air currents – into the sky and mate. All manner of birds, including gulls that are not usually insect-catchers, join the fray. They may not be as adept at catching insects as swallows and swifts but they do get a few beak-fulls.

Shark senses

Sharks have sensors that are the envy of military submarine designers, and one of them – probably the lateral line that can pick up pressure changes in the water – is capable of detecting large changes in atmospheric pressure. If the barometer is dropping dramatically, as it would before a hurricane, sharks head away from the coast where the water will be extremely turbulent and into deep water where they can ride out the storm.

Joey lore

A kangaroo baby, known locally as a 'joey', will take refuge in its mother's pouch if rain is on the way. More astonishing is the ability of the kangaroo mother to store her unborn embryos in a kind of 'suspended animation' during long, hot dry spells and then reanimate them when the rains come and the grass grows, providing ample food for mother and baby.

Too hot

When the temperature soars and an extended dry period is imminent, some animals opt out, a process known as 'aestivation'. At this time, they slow their heart rate and breathing, need less food and water and do not move, grow or eat. Reptiles in deserts, for example, use 90–95 per cent less energy during aestivation. Lungfish can aestivate for years, rather than months. They bury themselves in the mud of a shrinking lake, and when it dries out, they remain in this muddy cocoon until the lake fills again.

FACT
The longest period of dormancy ever recorded was a bacterium revived after spending 20–40 million years in the gut of a bee trapped in Dominican amber.

Too cold

When the temperature drops and food is scarce, one way to survive is to retire to a safe place and use as little energy as possible. This is 'hibernation' and some animals enter such as deep sleep they appear dead. North American chipmunks and ground squirrels are true, deep hibernators, and their body temperature during hibernation decreases to such an extent – below 4°C (40°F) – that if danger threatened they would have to warm up before being able to react. Many hibernators, however, do not 'sleep' for the entire winter, but wake up and 'shiver' to raise their body temperature slightly, or even go foraging if the weather is mild, and then go back to 'sleep' again.

Long dormancy

The animals that hibernate the longest include the marmot, with an 8-month hibernation period, and Belding's ground squirrel with 7–8 months. Ground squirrels in the southwest United States go into aestivation in summer to avoid the heat and sometimes do not emerge in autumn, but go straight into winter hibernation, making them the mammals with the longest dormancy period.

Insects hide in winter

Insects, being cold-blooded, would be seriously compromised if they had to live normally through winter, so most do not. They hide in rotten logs, under leaf litter, under the bark of trees and even in houses. Insects with the four-stage life cycle – egg, larva, pup and adult – do not hibernate, but spend the winter dormant in what is known as 'diapause'. It is a temporary halt in their life cycle, some spending the winter as larvae, others as pupae, before metamorphosing into adults the next spring. Social insects like wasps sacrifice the entire colony in the autumn, with only new queens surviving through the winter to start new colonies in spring.

Hibernating bears

Bears are 'super-hibernators'. Depending on what latitude and altitude they live at, they can hibernate for several days, like the black bears of Mexico, or over six months, like the grizzlies of Alaska.

Summer fat: *A hibernating bear's body temperature remains above 31°C (88°F), which is close to its active 37.7°C1 (00°F) body temperature. If disturbed in its den a bear can react immediately. It loses heat very slowly because it is well insulated with the body fat it put on during summer and with its thick coat.*

Winter lean: *Unlike other hibernators, bears do not eat, drink, urinate or defecate during hibernation. Waste products are recycled. The urea produced when fat is metabolised, for example, is broken down and the nitrogen released is used to build more proteins. So although bears lose body fat when hibernating they might actually gain lean-body mass. Overall, however, they do lose 15–30 per cent of their body weight during hibernation.*

ABOVE A queen hornet hibernating in damp wood.

Migration

The alternative to shutting down and hiding from the weather is to move temporarily to places where conditions are more favourable. Many animals migrate from one part of the world to another and from one climate to another, escaping from harsh winters, lack of food or lack of water. Movements are not only 'north to south', like those of snow geese that breed in the Arctic and winter near the Gulf of Mexico, but also 'east to west', like the migrations of jellyfish that follow the Sun in the lakes of Palau, and 'up to down' in the way that mountain quail spend summer in the mountains and winter in the sheltered valleys.

Bird migration

Birds make the most obvious migrations. When the time comes to move from their summer breeding places to their winter nesting sites, shortening day length and the dropping temperature are the cues to leave. Migration can occur in any month, but most movements are in spring and autumn. In temperate latitudes, the number of birds aloft during the migration period can vary up to a hundred-fold from one day to the next depending on the weather. Birds, it seems, can anticipate what will happen. Pigeons have been found to be sensitive to even small changes in air pressure, which would give them a clear indication of conditions ahead.

FACT

On 25 October 1998, a Peregrine Falcon being tracked by ornithologists in Florida was seen to change course in order to avoid an encounter with Hurricane Mitch. It was the first time a bird had been seen to react significantly in advance of a major weather system.

Follow the wind

Birds tend to fly when they have tail winds or when light winds are against them, and not when confronted with strongly opposing winds. Being led by the wind, they sometimes end up in the wrong place and have to alter their route. If they hit strong, unseasonable winds, they might even engage in a 'reverse migration' and retrace their steps.

High flying swans

On 9 December 1967, a flock of 30 Whooper Swans set off from Iceland and climbed rapidly to 8,230 m (27,000 feet), the height at which they were spotted by a commercial airline pilot over the Outer Hebrides and confirmed by Civil Air Traffic Control Radar Unit in Northern Ireland. They were riding a jetstream on a ridge of high pressure in the lower stratosphere at a ground speed of 139 km/h (86 mph) all the way to their destination in Loch Foyle, Northern Ireland. The atmospheric pressure at that height is one-third of that at the Earth's surface, oxygen concentration is 40 per cent less and the air temperature is an icy -48°C (-54.4°F) – a remarkable flight.

Hot air travellers

Eagles, hawks and vultures that use thermals – warm, rising air currents – to gain height without burning up energy during their everyday lives, also use rising columns of hot air while on migration. It has been estimated that North American Broad-winged hawks would use up their pre-migratory fat-load of 100 g (3.5 ounces) in just five days of flapping flight, but by spiralling up on one thermal and gliding down to the next, the stored fat lasts for 20 days, more than enough to fuel them on their 4,828 km (3,000-mile) spring journey from Central and South America to North America.

Locust swarms

Locusts ride on the warm winds associated with low-pressure and frontal systems. If they carry sufficient fat reserves they take off at sunset when the temperature is above 20°C (68°F) and are carried in upper level winds a distance of over 500 km (310 miles) to the places where rain has or is about to fall and vegetation is revitalised. If no green plants are encountered and conditions are favourable, they head off again. The strategy can have its flaws. In central Australia, the swarms can end up stranded in the middle of dried salt lakebeds, and West African locusts have been found in the middle of the Atlantic Ocean.

Swarms across the ocean

About two to three million years ago, a huge swarm of locusts in West Africa was whisked off by high altitude winds and carried right across the Atlantic to the Americas. Here, they evolved into several different locust species that now plague North America. A swarm made the same journey in October 1998, travelling from Africa to the Caribbean.

ABOVE An intense swarm of desert locusts in Keren, Ethiopia.

Plant forecasters

Chickweed, dandelions, bindweeds, wild indigo, clovers and tulips all close their flowers before rain. The bog pimpernel is very precise. When the relative humidity reaches 80 per cent, it closes its flower, giving rise to the rhyme: 'Pimpernel, pimpernel, tell me true; whether the weather be fine or no; no heart can think, no tongue can tell; the virtues of the pimpernel'. Flowers close their petals at the first sign of rain or mist to keep their pollen dry, but as the humidity drops they open up again. The scarlet pimpernel is known, therefore, as 'poor man's weather glass'.

Fungi and algae

The rainstar fungus opens when it is wet or humid and closes in dry weather. Mushrooms generally push up their fruiting bodies in damp weather, and seaweeds exposed on the seashore appear to swell during periods of high humidity prior to rain.

Adapting to the weather

Plants have leaves that are adapted to their climate. In tropical rainforests, for example, the trees have broad leaves with tips shaped like spouts that enable the rain to run off easily. In dry environments, plants such as cacti have nothing more than spines to avoid the loss of water. Similarly, conifers have spiky leaves that conserve water in cold climates. Grasses have tubular leaves to reduce water loss in high winds. Plants living in very windy places are generally stunted and have especially strong 'reaction wood' growing on the leeward side of the stem to help keep the plant standing.

FACT

A locust swarm can eat over 9,000 tonnes of vegetation per day – as much as 1,000 people can eat in the same time.

Weathering

It is not only plants and animals from the natural world that are affected by the weather. Rocks and minerals are broken down by the action of the wind, rain, snow and ice. This can take the form of mechanical or chemical weathering.

Mechanical weathering

Frost action: *Water freezes in cracks and crevices in rocks – the 'freeze-thaw cycle' – making them wider. Water expands about 8–11 per cent when it freezes, and the result is the formation of microfissures, cracks, flaking and spalling (chipping away).*

Thermal expansion: *Different minerals in rocks expand and contract at different rates. Dark minerals absorb heat more readily than light coloured ones. The stresses caused by the uneven heating by the Sun during the day and cooling at night can cause fractures and flaking.*

Wetting and drying: *Stone expands or contracts when it absorbs water or dries. The internal stresses can lead to flaking.*

Chemical weathering

Water, in the form of rain and fog (as well as rivers and sea), is the main agent in chemical weathering. It changes landscapes by dissolving minerals, or oxidising them so that they become 'rusted'.

Weathering in action

The 'Old Man of the Mountain' was a 12 m (40-foot) high granite rock formation in New Hampshire that inspired the children's story *The Great Stone Face* by Nathaniel Hawthorne. It was considered a state symbol, and appeared on coins and souvenirs. On 3 May 2003, however, it broke up and fell off because the bottom section succumbed to weathering, and now all that is left is a mountainside scar and a pile of rubble.

THE ENERGY OF
WEATHER

Wind turbines

Some of us think of 'wind farms' as a blight on the landscape, but we have been devising ways to harness the wind for centuries. If the energy from the wind is used directly as mechanical energy to cause a grindstone or water pump to operate it is known as a 'windmill'. If it is converted into electricity it is a 'wind generator'.

Earliest windmills

The first known windmills were constructed in Persia, for grinding grain in the seventh century BCE. Windmills of a similar design are also known from China, dated thirteenth century CE. The earliest known windmills in Europe were fixed windmills in twelfth-century Paris, which could not move to take advantage of wind direction. Later, windmill buildings were erected that could rotate, and windmills became important for power in mills, for threshing and for moving Archimedes screws in flood control or irrigation schemes.

Dutch windmills

In the Low Countries of Europe, the windmill came into its own by the fourteenth century. In Holland, for example, windmills were used to drive pumps that drained areas below sea level to claim new land. Jan Leeghwater undertook one of the first drainage operations in 1607, but the Archimedes screw used in those days failed to carry the water very far so rows of mills, known as *molengangen* or mill paces, were built. Each mill pumped the water to a higher reservoir until it was discharged into a river. A three-mill pace is known locally as a *molendriegangen* and a series of four mills known as a *molenviergangen*. One of the best preserved is at Kinderdijk in the Netherlands.

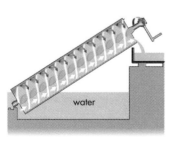

LEFT The Archimedes screw raises water through a simple but effective cylinder and screw action.

FACT
The first windmill adapted to produce electricity was built in Denmark in 1890.

Opening up the West

In the United States, the windmill was used mainly for pumping water from deep wells. For many years, wood or metal lattice towers, each with a multi-bladed wooden turbine on top, dominated the North American landscape. The large number of blades turn slowly but work well in low winds and are self-regulatory in strong winds. With this arrangement, water can be drawn from wells as deep as 366 m (1,200 feet).

Modern wind generators

These structures are categorised according to the position of the drive mechanism and the location of the turbine:

Horizontal axis wind turbines: *Old-fashioned windmills and the wind towers of the American farmlands are of this type, and it is the chosen system for modern wind farms. The drive shaft and generator are at the top of the tower and to work they must be pointing at the wind. Modern turbines are usually three-bladed, the blades stiffened to prevent them crashing into the tower. They are positioned facing the wind by computer-controlled servomotors.*

Vertical axis wind turbines: *These turbines have the main rotor shaft running vertically, with the generator and gearbox near the ground. This arrangement does not need to be pointing into the wind. There are three main types: the Darrieus Wind Turbine that resembles an eggbeater; the Giromill that features vertical blades with variable pitch; and the Savonius Wind Turbine that has two or three scoops like an anemometer.*

ABOVE A wind farm near Walla Walla, Washington State.

Giant wind turbines

Grandpa's Knob, in Vermont, was home to the world's first megawatt wind turbine. It was plugged into the local electricity grid in 1941. The 1.25-megawatt Smith-Putnam turbine worked successfully for 1,100 hours before one of the blades broke.

The world's largest turbines are now manufactured in northern Germany – the Enercon E112 is 186 m (610 feet) high, with a rotor diameter of 114 m (374 feet), and delivers 6 megawatts, and the REpower 5M is 183 m (600 feet) high, with a rotor diameter of 126 m (413 feet), and delivers 5 megawatts of electricity. One of Enercon's smaller turbines is used to power Australia's Mawson Bay research station in the Antarctic.

FACT
The wind turbine at the highest altitude currently is at 2,300 m (7,546 feet) on the Gütsch, a mountain near Andermatt, Switzerland.

Energy directly from the Sun

Our very existence depends on the Sun. Plants use the Sun's energy to create chemical energy during photosynthesis, and this is the basis not only of all foods on the planet, but also fossil fuels – oil, coal and peat – that were created sometime back in our geological past. We do not receive all the Sun's energy that reaches the Earth, however. The atmosphere absorbs about 19 per cent and clouds and other aerosols reflect 35 per cent back into space, while the rest reaches the surface.

Solar design

Using the Sun effectively is not new. The ancient Greeks and Romans built solar design features into their dwellings, as did the Pueblo villagers in the southwest of North America and the Incas of South America. In more recent times, the first houses with solar design features were built in the Allied-occupied Ruhr district of Germany after World War I. In the United States, the solar house was created almost by accident. Architect George F. Keck built a glass house for the 1933 Century of Progress Exposition in Chicago and noticed it warmed up significantly when the Sun was out. He then started to put more windows into south-facing walls in his regular buildings, and by 1940 acquired enough solar design knowledge to build a complete solar house for the real estate developer Howard Sloane. His efforts failed to catch the public imagination, however, until the oil crisis of 1973.

Trombe wall

The Trombe wall is a Sun-facing wall built from stone, concrete, adobe or water tanks that can store heat. It is separated by an airspace from insulated glazing and vents. The whole forms a large solar thermal collector. It was patented by Edward Morse in 1881, but only became popular from 1964, when it was taken up by engineer Felix Trombe and architect Jacque Michel. Sunlight shines through the double-glazing, warming the wall behind. Vents at the top and bottom of the air gap channel heat into the building's interior.

Capturing the Sun

Today, we have all manner of ways in which to harness energy from the Sun:

Solar cells: *Known also as photovoltaic (PV) or photoelectric cells, these convert sunlight directly into electricity. They were developed originally to power satellites in space, but are now used in such everyday instruments as calculators, solar-charging kits and illuminated traffic signs.*

Light absorption: *Solar cells rely on the light-absorbing properties of silicon and there are three types: monocrystalline, made by slicing thin wafers from high-purity crystal rods or boules; polycrystalline, made from molten silicon blocks sawed into plates; and amorphous, made from a super-thin film of silicon. Gallium arsenide is an alternative compound in solar cells.*

Solar water heating: *Heat from the Sun is used to warm water contained in glass panels. They are usually placed on the roof of a house, where water is pumped through pipes in the panel and heated by the Sun. The pipes are painted black to absorb more of the Sun's energy and connected to the building's central heating or the water heating system. In this way, the solar heating panel reduces the homeowner's electricity or energy bills. In northern Europe, 15–25 per cent of home heating energy can come from solar installations.*

Solar furnaces: *In Odeillo, France stands a large building with a vast array of mirrors, like a gigantic, shiny 'Hollywood Bowl'. An array of 63 mirrors (out of sight in the picture to the right) automatically track the movements of the Sun, reflecting it onto the main parabollic wall of mirrors. These mirrors then focus the Sun's rays onto the furnace, which is housed inside the central tower. This small space then heats up to 3,300°C (5,972°F). The Odeillo Furnace is operated solely for scientific experiments.*

ABOVE The Odeillo Furnace, France.

Stirling work

An alternative to rows of flat mirrors is a parabolic reflector. It focuses the Sun's rays to a point above the dish where a thermal collector captures the heat and transforms it into usable mechanical energy. This conversion is performed by a Stirling Engine or hot air engine, although a steam engine for generating electricity via turbines can also be utilised. The Reverend Robert Stirling invented the Stirling Engine, with assistance from his brother James, in 1816.

World's largest solar power plants

Peak power (MW)	Location	Peak power	Location
6.3	Mühlhausen, Germany	4	Gottleborn, Germany
5	Bürstadt, Germany	4	Hemau, Germany
5	Espenhain, Germany	3.9	Rancho Seco, California, USA
4.59	Springerville, Arizona, USA	3.3	Dingolfing, Germany
4	Geiseltalsee, Germany	3.3	Serre, Italy

World solar power production (end 2004)

Country	Total PV capacity (kW)	Country	Total PV capacity (kW)
Japan	1,131,991	Switzerland	23,100
Germany	794,000	Austria	19,180
United States	365,200	Mexico	18,182
Australia	52,300	Canada	13,884
The Netherlands	49,079	South Korea	9,892
Spain	37,000	United Kingdom	8,164
Italy	30,700	Norway	6,888
France	26,300		

H-Alpha Solar

A European idea for future solar harvesting proposes thin, flexible solar panels that are bonded into everyday fabrics. Solar panels could be woven into clothing in order to power up mobile phones. A tent's flysheet could charge batteries by day, providing campers with lights for the night. Scientists working on the pilot project H-Alpha Solar estimate that a letter-sized panel costing around £7 and woven into the back of a jacket would charge a mobile phone during a gentle summer stroll in the countryside.

FACT

A solar panel of just 1 sq m (10 square feet) of solar cells will provide enough power to run a 100-watt lightbulb. If the entire 9 million sq km (3.5 million square miles) of the unpopulated Sahara Desert were covered in solar panels, it would generate over 50 times the current energy needs of the entire world.

Solar towers

Another idea for the future is the 'solar tower'. It consists of a giant circular greenhouse with a tall, hollow tower at its centre. The principle is simple: the air in the greenhouse is warmed and the hot air rises rapidly in the tower in which turbines are located. It would work in countries with lots of sun and lots of space, such as Australia. Indeed, a 'solar tower power station' is intended to be operational in New South Wales, Australia, by 2008. To replace a 2,000-megawatt coal-fired power station, however, would require 10 of these proposed solar chimneys – but if successful this plant alone would mean 14 million tons less of greenhouse gases entering the atmosphere annually.

Like most ideas, the solar tower is not new. Muslim architects designed minarets as solar chimneys, and in 1931 a description for a 'solar chimney power station' featured in a book by German author Hans Günther. From 1975 Robert E. Lucier applied for patents for a working device, and between 1982 and 1989, a German-designed solar chimney model was erected in Manzanares, to the south of Madrid, Spain. Its chimney or tower was 10 m (33 feet) in diameter and 195 m (640 feet) high, and the glasshouse covered about 46,000 sq m (11 acres). It achieved a maximum output of 50 kilowatts.

A variation on the idea of the solar tower is the 'energy tower'. This uses the same principles of natural heat in a vertical space, but differs in that water is sprayed at the top of the chimney. The hot air evaporates the water but in the process cools down rapidly, and therefore becomes denser than the air outside. The dense air mass falls downwards in the tower, driving turbines at the bottom.

Solar pond

This is a low-tech solution to capturing the Sun's energy. A pond is filled with three layers of water, a less salty layer at the top and a saltier layer at the bottom. The middle layer is an insulating gradient zone, the salt content increasing with depth. This serves to trap heat in the lower layer from where it can be withdrawn. At 6 A.M. on 14 August 2002, the bottom layer of the El Paso Solar Pond in Texas was 62°C (143.6°F).

Solar cooker

In 1767, Swiss physicist and alpine traveler Horace-Bénédict de Saussure (1740–1799) invented a simple and relatively cheap way to cook food on a sunny day. He designed a solar box cooker. Today's version of this is an insulated box with a transparent top and a reflective lid. Cooking containers in the box are dark coloured and the inside walls are reflective. A solar box cooker can reach temperatures in excess of 50°C (122°F), not as hot as a standard oven, but useful when slow-cooking food over longer periods. In fact, food can be left to cook all day without burning.

A similar invention is the solar panel cooker, which consists of reflective panels that focus the Sun's rays on a black pot enclosed in a transparent, heat-resistant plastic bag. A version of this basic design is distributed in refugee camps where wood and other fuels are unavailable.

Solar lighting

Rather than light the interior of a building with costly electric lights, an alternative is to channel sunlight from the outside to the inside along fibre-optic light pipes connected to a parabolic reflector on the roof. The light provided is also more natural.

Ocean thermal energy conversion

This is a way of tapping into the temperature differences between the ocean's surface waters that are warmed by the Sun, and the colder, deeper waters. As heat flows from one to the other, a heat engine between the two layers extracts some of the heat and transforms it into usable energy. Within the Tropics of Capricorn and Cancer on either side of the Equator, the temperature difference between the two layers can be 20°C (36°F), but such a small difference makes energy extraction difficult. Scientists continue to work on the process, however, because the oceans are vast – over 70 per cent of the Earth's surface – and the potential is enormous.

GLOBAL
WEATHER
CHANGE

Climate change

The Earth has followed natural cycles of cooling and warming since it first began. These changes can last for just a few years or for millions of years. Global warming, for example, is thought to have occurred during the early Jurassic period about 180 million years ago, a time when the dinosaurs dominated the world. Average global temperature was thought to have risen by 5–10°C (9–18°F). In the geologically recent past, the planet was locked in an Ice Age, and some climatologists believe we are still experiencing the tail end of that phenomenon, although technically we are said to be in an 'interglacial' period.

Melting Snowball Earth

The greenhouse effect was thought to have broken the icy grip of Snowball Earth about 550 million years ago. Previously the planet had undergone the most severe period of glaciation, with all the world's oceans freezing over to a depth of 2 km (1.2 miles). Rocks that would

ABOVE A glacier calving icebergs into the sea in Patagonia, Argentina.

normally lock up carbon dioxide (CO_2) were buried in snow and ice, so CO_2 levels rose to 350 times those experienced today. The resulting greenhouse effect caused the average global temperature to rise to over 50°C (122°F), and the global ice sheets melted.

It's getting warmer... but why?

Today, climate change means one thing to most people, for the words 'global warming' are on everybody's lips... but is global warming real or not? The answer depends on whom you talk to. The world's experts, in the form of the United Nations Intergovernmental Panel on Climate Change and the national science institutions of all the G8 nations, Brazil, India and China, have reached a consensus that the average global temperature has risen by 0.4 to 0.8°C (0.72–1.44°F) since the nineteenth century, and that most of the warming for the past 50 years is attributable to humankind.

Projecting into the future, they believe that by 2100 the global temperature will increase by 1.5–5.8°C (2.7–10.44°F). This could result in:

A rise in sea level *and a dramatic change in precipitation patterns throughout the world, submerging many low-lying island nations and leaving up to three-quarters of the world's population at risk from drought or flood.*

Changes in patterns of agriculture *and depleted crop yields. Some predictions state 30 million more people will go hungry because of climate change by 2050.*

Extinction: *More than 1 million species of plants and animals by 2050. In order to assess the impact of climate change on wildlife, scientists examined six biodiversity-rich areas of the globe (20 per cent of the planet's land area) and the expected distribution of 1103 species living in them. Using computer models, in which they loaded data from the Intergovernmental Panel on Climate Change, they found that up to 37 per cent of species would be extinct by 2050.*

Climate change definitions

Global warming: *Global warming is the average increase in the temperature of the atmosphere and oceans. Today, it also encompasses the impact of human activities, such as the burning of fossil fuels to heat our homes and power our industries.*

Greenhouse effect: *The Earth is like a greenhouse. The atmosphere contains gases, such as carbon dioxide, that behave like the glass in a greenhouse. They let the Sun's rays in, but prevent heat from escaping. Quite naturally, the Earth's surface is kept about 30–33°C (54–59.4°F) warmer than it would without greenhouse gases. A build up of carbon dioxide in the atmosphere from burning fossil fuels and removing forests is thought to be contributing to that effect.*

Greenhouse gases: *The natural greenhouse gases are water vapour, carbon dioxide, methane, nitrous oxide and chlorofluorocarbons, as well as various fluoroethanes, fluoromethanes and fluorides. It is difficult to quantify the effect of each greenhouse gas, but it is said that water vapour contributes about two-thirds of the greenhouse effect. Carbon dioxide levels are 3–7 per cent.*

Myth or reality?

A small but vociferous group of scientists believe the threat is exaggerated, and that we are passing through an uncomfortable period in a lengthy, natural climate cycle, caused by factors such as wobbles in the Earth's orbit. Astrophysicists, for example, argue that the natural warming and cooling cycles of the Earth, including the present warming one, are due to natural oscillations in solar activity. It is certainly true that the Earth has passed through other periods of global warming (see chart on page 72). It has even been argued that the dinosaurs may have died out in a period of global warming, brought on by carbon dioxide that was pumped into the atmosphere after a series of massive volcanic explosions in Siberia 251 million years ago.

Carbon dioxide (CO$_2$)

This is the main gas we breathe out during respiration and that green plants and algae utilise during photosynthesis. Without any major disturbances, the Earth would reach a natural equilibrium of atmospheric gases, with the trees in great forests and the phytoplankton in the ocean acting as 'sinks' for the carbon dioxide that animals produce. The balance can swing the wrong way quite naturally, however, when a large volcano erupts, or artificially when humans burn fossil fuels.

Methane

Methane hydrates are much more effective greenhouse gases than carbon dioxide. These gases, stored in ocean sediments and polar permafrost, can be released in large volumes. Such volumes may have caused the rapid warming and subsequent extinctions 55 million years ago.

Globally, the rearing of livestock, natural gas, rice paddies, landfill sites, gas flaring and coal use and extraction put 450 million tons of methane into our atmosphere each year.

Cows account for a substantial part of the methane in the atmosphere. Brazil and India have the largest cattle herds in the world and subsequently contribute more methane than any other countries. Brazil's 160 million head of cattle, for example, produces about 30 per cent of its methane.

FACT
Worldwide, coal-burning power stations, automobile exhausts, and industrial plants – all of which burn fossil fuels – spew 22 million tons of carbon dioxide and other greenhouse gases into our atmosphere each year.

Moving ocean currents

Heat is transported from the Equator to the Poles not only by the atmosphere, but also by ocean currents. Warm water moves at the surface and cold water deeper down. One section of this circulation is the Gulf Stream, which transports warm water from the Caribbean northward, with a sub-branch known as the North Atlantic Drift warming the waters of northwest Europe.

Evaporation of this warm water in the North Atlantic causes it to become more saline and to cool. The cooler water sinks and returns southward at depth. Global warming, and the subsequent melting of Greenland's ice sheet and glaciers, could interrupt this warm-cold ocean circulation, destroying the Gulf Stream and causing a serious drop in temperature in northern Europe.

Looking back

In order to compare the average global air temperature and the composition of the atmosphere today with that of yesteryear, scientists can call on several sources:

Tree rings: *Record the annual growth of a tree, but also reflect the weather during the course of the year. These can be used to look at weather up to 2,000 years ago. Wide rings denote warm weather favourable to growth; narrow rings denote cold weather most likely dominated.*

Ice core samples: *Drilled from glaciers and ice sheets, these reveal what the climate was like when the ice was formed and can reveal climates over 100,000 years old. Small bubbles in the ice are tiny time capsules of air that can be sampled and analysed. They show that there was less carbon dioxide in the atmosphere during the Ice Age than there is today.*

Amber: *The fossilised resin from conifer trees often has trapped insects, plant material and bubbles of air. Solidified amber preserves these indicators of a past climate.*

FACT
Dust and volcanic aerosols spewed into the atmosphere during the 1816 eruption of Mt Tambora in Indonesia, causing North America's 'year without a summer'.

The evidence

Since 1750, before the Industrial Revolution, the concentration of carbon dioxide has increased by 31 per cent. During the same period, the increase for methane has been 149 per cent. Ice core sampling indicates this is the highest rise in 650,000 years, and geological evidence indicates that these levels were last reached about 40 million years ago, coincidentally the time during the Eocene period when grasses and even-toed ungulates were evolving rapidly. This is the animal group that includes cows!

Cool years

Massive volcanic eruptions, such as Krakatoa and Tambora, cooled the atmosphere by sending ash and sulphurous gases up to 32 km (20 miles) high into the middle stratosphere where they were carried right around the world. Sulphates combined with water to form droplets of sulphuric acid, which reflect sunlight away from the Earth's surface. In recent times, Mexico's 1981 eruption of El Chichon and the 1991 eruption of Pinatuba in the Philippines cooled the atmosphere by 0.6°C (1°F) for a couple of years.

Hot year

According to NASA's Goddard Institute for Space Studies, the year 2005 was the warmest on record. Other institutions, such as the World Meteorological Organisation and the UK's Climatic Research Unit at the University of East Anglia, England, consider that 1998 still holds the record.

Urban heat islands

Villages, towns, and cities are significantly warmer than surrounding rural areas, and as they grow so does their average air temperature. This phenomenon is known as 'urban heat islands,' and on a hot summer's day a city can be 1–6°C (2–10°F) warmer than the countryside nearby. It also means that rainfall 32–64 km (20–40 miles) downwind of a city can be 28 per cent greater. Causes are multiple. Construction materials such as concrete and asphalt have replaced vegetation and retain more heat. Automobiles, air-conditioning units and industry contribute heat, and high levels of pollution can invoke a local greenhouse effect.

FACT
The first record of urban heat islands was made in 1820 by British meteorologist and pharmacist Luke Howard (1772–1864). In his *Climate of London*, he described how the centre of London at night was '3.7° warmer' than in the country. He attributed the difference in temperature to the greater use of fuel to keep warm in the city.

Hot and cold cities

Heat islands can be a problem for cities in hot climates, especially in summer when elderly people and children are at risk of dying from excessive heat. It also has a financial angle: Los Angeles is reported to consume an additional $100 million dollars of energy per year to power air-conditioning and refrigeration units. Meanwhile Chicago, in a colder climate, benefits from the heat island effect during winter.

Canyon effect

Tall buildings in high-rise cities, such as New York City, have many surfaces for reflecting and absorbing sunlight. They also block the wind, preventing cooling convection currents from forming. In this way, they also contribute to urban heat islands.

Smog

This is very dense and visible air pollution, usually associated with large cities. Gray smog was once common in London and New York, and was caused by the burning of coal and fuel oil that produced soot, other particulates and sulphur compounds. Brown smogs are often seen in Los Angeles and Denver, and are caused mainly by vehicles. Nitrous oxide from the exhausts of millions of automobiles, vans and trucks combines with oxygen to form the brown gas nitrogen dioxide. In addition, the nitrous oxides and hydrocarbons from exhausts react with sunlight to form a photochemical smog.

Smog casualties

Smog has harmful effects on people, including irritation to the eyes and respiratory tract, and can be serious enough to kill people. The London smog of 1952 accounted for over 4,000 deaths, and a smog in Donora, Pennsylvania, from 26 to 31 October 1948, resulted in an estimated 7,000 hospitalisations from asphyxiation and 20 deaths in a town with no more than 14,000 inhabitants. It was considered the worst air pollution disaster in the United States.

ABOVE A view of the smog that prevails most of the time over Mexico City.

Ozone holes

Ozone (O_3) occurs naturally in the highest ranges of the atmosphere when ultraviolet radiation (sunlight) strikes the stratosphere, splitting atmospheric oxygen molecules (O_2) to atomic oxygen (O). The atomic oxygen quickly combines with further oxygen molecules to form ozone. Life on Earth could not survive without the protection ozone gives from solar radiation.

Any influence that ozone depletion has on climate change is thought to be minimal. An increase in atmospheric carbon dioxide, while causing warming in the lower parts of the atmosphere (troposphere), should cool the stratosphere. This would lead to an increase in ozone there and a filling of the ozone holes.

Acid rain and radioactive rain

Acid rain refers to any precipitation that has a pH of less than 5 (i.e., acidic). It is formed when sulphur and nitrogen compounds from industrial installations, such as fossil fuel power stations, are oxidised to form dilute sulphuric and nitric acids. Acid rain is harmful to soils and waterways, and to the creatures that live on or in them. Many lakes affected by acid rain have very clear water, as if pure, but this anomaly simply disguises the fact that they are totally dead.

In 1986 at Chernobyl, Ukraine, a nuclear power plant exploded and clouds of radioactive particles were flung into the air. The winds and radioactive rains carried the plume of fall-out to parts of the then Soviet Union, Eastern Europe, Scandinavia, the UK and the United States.

The Kyoto Protocol

On 16 February 2005, the Kyoto Protocol, aimed at stemming carbon dioxide emissions and limiting global warming, came into force. The treaty has been ratified by 141 countries, accounting for 55 per cent of the world's greenhouse emissions.

Index

Picture credits

The publishers would like to thank the following for permission to reproduce images.
  NOAA: pp. 18, 23, 32, 34, 37, 59, 63, 64, 68, 69, 93, 99, 101, 105
  NASA: pp. 7, 26, 28, 82, 87
  Science Photo Library: pp. 8, 13, 50, 78, 80, 88, 108, 112, 115, 118, 127, 132, 139
  Richard Burgess (illustrator): pp. 10, 20, 38, 47, 56, 72, 75, 122
  John "Cloudman" Day: p.43; Photolibrary.com: p. 53; Patrick Brown: p.70; Stan Celestian:
  p. 95; Sparktography.com: p. 124

Websites

National Oceanic & Atmospheric Administration (USA) http://www.noaa.gov

National Hurricane Center (USA) http://www.nhc.noaa.gov

National Weather Service (USA) http://www.nws.noaa.gov

Federal Emergency Management Agency (USA) http://www.fema.gov

NASA Global Hydrology & Climate Center (USA) http://www.ghcc.msfc.nasa.gov

The Meteorological Office (UK) http://www.metoffice.gov.uk

B.B.C. Weather (UK) http://www.bbc.co.uk/weather

Australian Bureau of Meteorology (Aus.) http://www.bom.gov.au

European Organisation for the Exploitation of Meteorological Satellites (Eur.)
http://www.eumetsat.int

European Space Agency (Eur.) http://www.esa.int/esaCP/index.html